SINKING
THE
SULTANA

SINKING THE SULTANA

A CIVIL WAR STORY OF IMPRISONMENT, GREED, AND A DOOMED JOURNEY HOME

SALLY M. WALKER

CANDLEWICK PRESS

Copyright © 2017 by Sally M. Walker

Front cover illustration used with permission of the Hartford Steam Boiler
Inspection and Insurance Company; back cover photograph courtesy of
the Cincinnati History Library and Archives

Interior image credits appear on page 192.
Maps on pages 2, 26, 68, 114 and diagrams on pages 47 and 107
copyright © 2017 by Karen Minot

First edition 2017

Library of Congress Catalog Card Number pending
ISBN 978-0-7636-7755-8

17 18 19 20 21 22 APS 10 9 8 7 6 5 4 3 2 1

Printed in Humen, Dongguan, China

This book was typeset in Bulmer.

Candlewick Press
99 Dover Street
Somerville, Massachusetts 02144

visit us at www.candlewick.com

In memory of those lost in the Sultana *disaster,*
and in tribute to all people who aid survivors
in need — anytime, anyplace

CONTENTS

ROLL CALL

More than twenty-five hundred people are part of the *Sultana*'s story. They include army and navy personnel, paroled prisoners of war, civilian passengers, steamboat crews, medical personnel, and the civilians of Memphis, Tennessee. All their stories are interesting, but to include everyone in this telling would require a book hundreds of pages long. Some individuals made decisions that affected thousands of lives. The following people tell various parts of this particular *Sultana* story.

OFFICERS IN THE UNITED STATES ARMY:
DEPARTMENT OF MISSISSIPPI

Major General Napoleon Dana

Brigadier General Morgan Smith

Colonel Reuben Hatch

Captain George Williams

Captain Frederic Speed

Captain William Kerns

CREW ON THE *SULTANA*

James Cass Mason — captain

George Kayton — pilot

Henry Ingraham — pilot

Nathan Wintringer — chief engineer

Samuel Clemens — second engineer

William Gambrel — first clerk

William Rowberry — first mate

CIVILIAN PASSENGERS ON THE *SULTANA*

The Annis family: Harvey (invalided out of the army), Ann,
and their daughter Isabella

Seth Hardin Jr. and Hannah Hardin, his bride

Daniel McLeod, Eighteenth Illinois Infantry (invalided out of the army)

Nine members of the Spikes family, including Samuel, Elethia,
Susan, and DeWitt

PAROLED UNION PRISONERS OF WAR

Simeon Chelf — Sixth Kentucky Cavalry

Ben Davis — Seventh Kentucky Cavalry

Michael Dougherty — Thirteenth Pennsylvania Cavalry

J. Walter Elliott — Tenth Indiana Volunteer Infantry and
Forty-Fourth Regiment U.S. Colored Troops

John Clark Ely — 115th Ohio Volunteer Infantry

Stephen Gaston — Ninth Indiana Volunteer Cavalry

Robert Hamilton — Third Tennessee Cavalry

Nicholas Karns — Eighteenth Ohio Infantry

Albert King — 100th Ohio Infantry

Hugh Kinser — Fiftieth Ohio Infantry

William Lugenbeal — 135th Ohio Infantry

Jesse Martin — Thirty-Fifth Indiana Infantry

Joseph Mayes — Fortieth Indiana Infantry

William McFarland — Forty-Second Indiana Infantry

James Payne — 124th Indiana Infantry

Jacob Rush — Third Ohio Cavalry

PROLOGUE

APRIL 27, 1865, 2:30 A.M.

The second time a crewman knocked on the door of her husband's quarters in the middle of the night, Frances Ackley knew something serious had happened. Less than half an hour earlier, her husband, Charles, the executive officer on the gunboat USS *Tyler,* had been summoned to the deck. Upon returning to their berth, he told Frances that a boat was burning on the Mississippi River but it was too far upriver for his men to render assistance.

News of a steamboat fire would not have surprised Frances. Coal fueled a steamboat's furnaces, so fires were not unusual. Also, the effects of the recently ended Civil War still shook the United States. She knew that boats often caught fire during river battles. For the past three years, Charles had served in the United States Navy on gunboats that patrolled the Mississippi River and its tributaries, on guard against boats and soldiers belonging to the Confederacy. But that night on the *Tyler,* which was docked in Memphis, Tennessee, Frances hadn't heard any gunfire.

Frances rose from the berth and dressed. Leaving their baby soundly asleep, she joined her husband on the *Tyler*'s deck. A distant orange glow flickered against the cloudy sky. But it was the sounds nearby that distressed her. From all directions in the river, men screamed for help.

Just a few hours earlier, several officers from the *Tyler* had visited the steamboat *Sultana* while it was refueling at a coal barge near Memphis. More than two thousand Union soldiers, recently released from prisoner-of-war camps, crowded its decks. The *Tyler*'s men had offered the ill, half-starved soldiers words of encouragement and wished them a safe journey. Everyone on board the *Tyler* knew that only a boat heavily loaded with people could account for the number of men and women in the river.

Charles ordered the *Tyler*'s two cutters, or small boats, lowered to the water. Frances stepped toward the second cutter. Charles tried to stop her, but Frances, determined to help, pulled free and climbed aboard.

Frances's boat floated toward a drift of wood. Men, sobbing with pain, clung to the dead branches. Standing in the bow, Frances reached out with a boat hook and snagged a man's shirt. She pulled him toward the cutter. As others lifted him on board, she reached for the next man. Dozens more floated past, out of reach. The Mississippi River had become a living nightmare. And it had only just begun.

CHAPTER I
STEAMBOATS A-COMIN'

THE CROOKEDEST RIVER

The name "Mississippi" comes from two words in the Ojibwe language, *gichi* and *ziibi,* which mean "a big river." And the Mississippi River is big. During its 2,350-mile-long journey from northern Minnesota to the Gulf of Mexico, the rivers and streams of two Canadian provinces and thirty-one states funnel into its channel. The author and riverboat pilot Samuel Langhorne Clemens (who wrote under the pen name Mark Twain) believed that the Mississippi's looping meanders made it the "crookedest river in the world." One leg of its journey, he declared, "used up one thousand three hundred miles to cover the same ground that the crow would fly over in six hundred and seventy-five."

Hundreds of years before Europeans arrived in the New World, the Chickasaw people navigated southern portions of the Mississippi in dugout canoes. The Ojibwe paddled birch-bark canoes along the river's northernmost reaches. In 1541, Spanish explorer Hernando de Soto and his men reached the river's east

For thousands of years, people from many different cultures have lived near the Mississippi River and traveled its waters in a variety of floating vessels.

bank, near the area now known as Memphis, Tennessee. They were the first Europeans to see the river that far inland, and they marveled at its powerful current: "The water was alwaies muddie: there came downe the river continually many trees and timber, which the force of the water and streame brought downe." Sometimes, so much mud and sand are suspended in the river that the water looks like cocoa.

During the next two hundred years, explorers, traders, and then settlers from the east spread into the western frontier. Flatboats became a common sight on the vast western river system created

Flatboats, which could be up to sixty feet long and ten to twenty-five feet wide, provided a convenient way to travel downstream, but navigating them upstream was difficult, if not impossible.

by the Mississippi River and its tributaries. These large, rectangular boats accommodated settlers and their belongings — even their horses and cows. But flatboats worked best as a one-way vehicle. While they easily floated downriver, their blocky shape made upstream travel against the Mississippi's current (which ranges from one to three miles per hour) difficult, if not impossible.

Keelboats, often as large as flatboats, soon became a popular choice of transportation. Their tapered bow and stern made maneuvering upstream easier. Even so, overcoming the current required the manpower of several crewmen. In shallow water, the crew propelled the boat upriver with long poles pushed into the river bottom. In deep water, they tied one end of a rope to the boat and towed the vessel from the shore. During much of the 1800s, most of the land along the Mississippi was a "trackless forest." Towing a keelboat meant trudging "through the tangled undergrowth and miry swamps . . . inhabited only by the snake and the alligator." Manpower wasn't strong enough for fast upstream travel.

FULL STEAM AHEAD

To a businessman, time and labor cost money. For a businessman from the western states, a boat that could reduce the transportation time of people and goods — lumber, iron, stone, sugar, and cotton — to eastern markets would be a gold mine. In 1810, Robert Fulton and Robert Livingston decided that steamboats (which already carried passengers in the bays on the East Coast and on New York's Hudson River) would be a profitable venture for

A keelboat was steered with a rudder at the stern. When traveling upriver, keelboat men used poles, like the one seen lying across this boat's hull, to overcome the current that faced them.

western rivers. They hired Nicholas Roosevelt to build a steamboat in Pittsburgh, Pennsylvania.

On October 20, 1811, the *New Orleans,* named after the Louisiana city that would be its homeport, departed Pittsburgh under Roosevelt's command. The boat's cylindrical iron boiler contained water that, when heated, provided the steam that powered its engine. The engine turned a large paddle wheel at the stern. The turning buckets, or flat paddles of the wheel, pushed against

Skeptics doubted whether the New Orleans *had the power for long-distance trips upriver.*

the water and propelled the boat. Black smoke belched from the steamboat's chimney as it steamed west along the Ohio River heading for southern Illinois. There, it would cruise into the Mississippi River and head south for New Orleans.

During the voyage, the *New Orleans* periodically stopped to collect wood for fuel. (Later, coal would replace wood as steamboat fuel.) It impressed onlookers with speeds as fast as eight to ten miles per hour. The *New Orleans* overcame setbacks such as shallow water and a shipboard fire. Despite these delays, the steamboat arrived at the city of New Orleans on January 12, 1812, proving that a steamboat could make the long journey. For two years, the *New Orleans* ran regularly scheduled trips between the cities of New Orleans and Natchez, Mississippi. Its career ended in 1814, when it struck a stump in the river, sprang a leak, and sank.

Yet stumbling blocks still remained for cost-efficient steamboat travel on western rivers. One of them was the shape of the boat's hull, or frame. Large oceangoing ships have a hull that extends deep beneath the water's surface. The deep hull stabilizes the ships against waves, winds, and currents. But the depth of western rivers constantly changes. It rises and falls as much as fifty feet according to the season and climatic conditions. To successfully navigate rivers with such large fluctuations, western steamboats needed a hull with a shallower draft (the depth of the hull beneath the water's surface) than oceangoing ships, even when fully loaded.

Power was another problem. The *New Orleans* and steamboats that were used along the East Coast contained low-pressure steam engines. But over the long distance from southern ports to

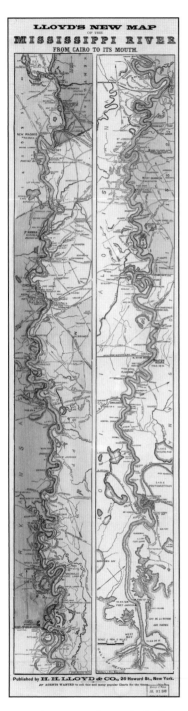

For safety, a steamboat pilot had to know the Mississippi River's meandering channel.

northern cities such as Cincinnati and Pittsburgh, a low-pressure engine was no match for currents of the Mississippi and Ohio Rivers, which could be as fast as eight to ten miles an hour. A low-pressure steam engine also lacked the power to push through mud or to barge over a sandbar should the boat become mired. Western boatbuilders wanted steamboats that suited western rivers. They decided to design and manufacture the boats they needed themselves.

STEAMING IN THE WEST

By the time he was a teenager, riverboats were in Henry Shreve's blood. He bought his own keelboat when he was twenty-two years old and regularly traveled the Ohio and Mississippi Rivers. An expert navigator and captain, Shreve knew the rivers' challenges and believed steamboats were the boat of the future. He'd seen Fulton's *New Orleans* and had ideas for improvement. To implement these ideas, Shreve collaborated with Daniel French, an inventor who had patented a high-pressure steam engine that generated a lot more power than low-pressure engines. In 1814, French built the *Enterprise,* a sixty- to seventy-foot-long steamboat with a high-pressure steam engine.

Shreve captained the boat from Pittsburgh to New Orleans. Early in 1815, the *Enterprise* steamed upriver from New Orleans to Pittsburgh, the first steamboat to do so. Including its stops at various ports to load and unload freight, it made the trip in fifty-four days — a greatly reduced time compared with the almost three months posted by Fulton and Livingston's *New Orleans* and its low-pressure engine.

By then, Shreve had ideas for an even better boat. In 1816, he built the *Washington*. Its eighty-foot-long central cabin, where passengers socialized and dined, was longer than the entire *Enterprise*. But it was Shreve's changes to the boat's machinery that made it special. He modified French's high-pressure engine, but, in a new construction twist, he installed a flat roof above the engine, running the length of the hull. This created a main deck, just slightly above the water.

Then Shreve came up with an eyebrow-raising innovation: he put the *Washington*'s cylindrical steam boiler up on the main deck, in the middle area of the boat. He also modified the boiler so it could be installed in a horizontal position rather than vertically, as was typical. By relocating the massive boiler, he was able to reduce the boat's draft, or the depth of water it required, eliminating the problem of running aground in shallow river depths. After test runs on the Ohio River, Shreve captained the *Washington* from Pittsburgh to New Orleans. On its return north, it completed the 1,350-mile trip from New Orleans to Louisville in a record time of twenty-five days — a *huge* improvement over the three to four months that it took a keelboat to travel the same route. The *Washington*'s success impressed other boatbuilders, and it quickly became the prototype for all western steamboats.

Yet traveling on the *Washington* could be dangerous. On June 9, 1816, seven people on board died when one of its boilers exploded. The *Washington*'s explosion was the first high-pressure-boiler explosion. Many more followed.

Afloat or mired in the river bottom, fallen tree trunks and branches posed a serious threat to the hulls of boats that traveled on western rivers.

Despite the risk, high-pressure engines were the wave of the future. People wanted power and speed, and steamboats supplied both. By 1819, thirty-one steamboats ran on western rivers. That number increased to about 450 by 1840, and many of them traveled one hundred miles per day. By 1848, the network of western rivers had become a steamboat water-highway of more than fifteen thousand miles.

Builders quickly met consumer demands: between 1845 and 1855, boatyards in Ohio, Indiana, Pennsylvania, and Kentucky produced more than one hundred steamboats per year. The secretary of war's report to the president of the United States estimated that in 1855, there were 2,596 steamboats on western rivers. Boatyards in Cincinnati, Pittsburgh, and Louisville bustled with activity as workers flocked to the iron foundries, lumber mills, and machine shops that constructed different parts of the boats. Boatbuilders increased the number of engines in a steamboat from one to two. They added power by enlarging the boilers and installing more of them on large boats. The hold, or storage area beneath the main deck, and the large main deck of these new steamboats offered ample cargo space. Additional decks — built on top of the main deck like the layers of a cake — accommodated dozens more passengers. Smoking chimneys and blaring steam whistles were the sights and sounds of business as usual on all of the large western rivers. And then everything changed.

As 1860 drew to a close, opposing views about economic issues around the country, the ownership of enslaved African Americans, and the expansion of slavery seemed irreconcilable. The federal government and states in the northern part of the country wanted slavery's expansion stopped; southern states did not. In November, Abraham Lincoln's election to the presidency escalated tensions between the opposing points of view. Within three months, seven southern states seceded from the Union and declared themselves the Confederate States of America. On April 12, 1861, in South Carolina, Confederate forces in Charleston Harbor fired on besieged federal Fort Sumter and captured it the next day. On April 15, President Lincoln issued a proclamation. In it, he called for the Union's state militias to enroll seventy-five thousand men "in order to suppress" the actions taken by the seven states that had seceded. By June, four more states had seceded and joined the Confederacy. Northern and Southern armies swelled as more men enlisted. Small skirmishes occurred in Virginia. In July, Union and Confederate forces met in a larger battle in the fields at Bull Run, in Manassas, Virginia. After that, the United States of America plunged into civil war.

CHAPTER 2

OFF TO WAR

MEN ENROLLED in the Union army for many reasons. Some answered President Lincoln's proclamation to suppress the states that seceded and prevent them from permanently dividing the United States. Others enlisted to help abolish slavery. The promise of a monthly paycheck lured more. The men came from many walks of life. They ranged widely in age. Some joined the infantry, while others served on horseback in the cavalry. While the men's motivation, backgrounds, and branch of service may have differed, they had one thing in common: all were ready to risk their lives for their country.

CALLED TO ARMS

Eighteen-year-old Michael Dougherty, who had immigrated to the United States from Ireland less than four years earlier, answered his new country's call to arms in August 1862. A good rider, he enlisted in Pennsylvania's 117th Regiment, Thirteenth Cavalry, also known as the Irish Dragoons. Stationed in Virginia,

As did many immigrants, Michael Dougherty answered his new nation's call to arms and enlisted.

Dougherty's horseback-mounted regiment patrolled against enemy raids and routed out rebel cavalry. In February 1863, after a skirmish, Dougherty was riding back toward camp. Without warning, a large force of heavily armed Confederates attacked the Dragoons. Dougherty's horse was shot from under him. He and fifty others were captured and taken to Libby Prison, a prisoner-of-war camp in Richmond, Virginia.

Two months later, Dougherty was paroled in a procedure that released one imprisoned Union soldier in exchange for one imprisoned Confederate soldier of equal rank. The paroled soldiers were required to promise that they would not fight again until the two armies formally acknowledged the exchange and the official paperwork was completed. During the early years of the war, the parole process usually took a couple of weeks or less. Within days of his parole, Dougherty was back in the saddle.

In October 1863, the Dragoons were again attacked. On October 12, under deadly fire, Dougherty led his company in a charge across an open field and drove the rebel forces away.

Dougherty and his comrades defended their new position "for several hours against repeated attacks, thus preventing the enemy from flanking the position of Union forces." However, Confederate forces ultimately won the engagement, and Dougherty was recaptured. This time, he remained imprisoned for more than a year.

BROTHERS

Robert Hamilton was born and raised in Tennessee, which seceded from the Union in June 1861, the last Confederate state to do so. He lived on the family farm, southwest of Knoxville, with his parents, five brothers, and two sisters. Robert opposed secession, but he hadn't been old enough to vote against it. The Hamilton family, like many residents of eastern Tennessee, did not support the Confederate government. These citizens remained loyal to the United States and showed their support by establishing more than forty Tennessee Union regiments. More than thirty-one thousand Tennessee men joined the Union army.

Although their family lived in a state that had seceded, Robert Hamilton and his brothers joined the Union army.

In 1862, Robert and his brothers John and Henry enlisted in the Tennessee infantry—but they had to travel to the pro-Union state of Kentucky to do it. (Confederate forces often harassed the local pro-Union residents. Some of the Hamiltons' pro-Union neighbors were even arrested.) By 1864, the three brothers had transferred into Company F of the Third Tennessee Cavalry. John Hamilton, the oldest, served as the regiment's farrier. Henry, the youngest, became a sergeant. Robert was a private.

In February 1864, Robert Hamilton became ill with smallpox and was furloughed home to recuperate. While he was recovering, Union troops stopped at the Hamiltons' farm and requisitioned Robert Hamilton's favorite horse, a roan mare, for the army. Reluctantly, he unharnessed the animal and watched as "one of the men mounted her and rode her off without any saddle." The soldiers did not pay Hamilton for his horse, and he never saw her again.

Before the end of May, Robert Hamilton had fully recovered and rejoined his brothers with the Third Tennessee Cavalry.

On September 23, 1864, the Third Cavalry charged across cornfields toward Athens, Alabama, to drive away Confederate forces that were destroying a railroad track. Before nightfall, they had engaged in four skirmishes, advancing and holding the line. The Hamilton brothers took shelter inside a fort for the night. Early the next morning, Confederate general Nathan Forrest arrived and surrounded the fort with eight to ten thousand cavalry and artillery troops, vastly outnumbering the Union soldiers inside. Forrest met with the fort's commander and demanded surrender. Faced with insurmountable odds and a likely bloodbath, the commander chose to preserve the lives of his men, and he surrendered. Robert, John, and Henry Hamilton and hundreds of their comrades in the Third Tennessee Cavalry became prisoners of war.

THE BUGLER

Thirteen-year-old Stephen Gaston was determined to join the army. Because of his age, Gaston could not enlist as a soldier. Rather than join the army in one of the other roles allowed for underage men—a water carrier or a hospital attendant, for example—he enlisted in the Ninth Indiana Volunteer Cavalry in October 1863 as a musician. Even though he wouldn't carry a gun at first, his duty as a bugler was important. He soon learned to blow as many as fifty or more different signals. When the Ninth Indiana Cavalry advanced in a thunder of

Stephen Gaston, the bugler for the Ninth Indiana Volunteer Cavalry, probably carried a bugle that looked like this one. The name of the young man in this picture is unknown.

hoofbeats, Gaston's bugle blared a pattern of notes that communicated battle instructions such as advance, trot, gallop, charge, and retreat. Daily, his bugle woke the men in the morning and called them to meals and roll call. It ordered them to strike tents and told them when to march. Gaston's bugle sounded a special call to sick soldiers, reminding them to get their medicine. A final trumpet call from his bugle sent the men to bed at night.

In the summer of 1864, Gaston and the Ninth Indiana Cavalry marched to Tennessee, and then to Alabama.

At the end of September, Gaston's regiment gamely defended the railroad tracks near a small Union fort called Sulphur Branch Trestle, not far from the place where the Hamilton brothers were captured. General Forrest's forces attacked Gaston's regiment on Sunday, September 25. By day's end, two hundred Union soldiers were dead; nine hundred others surrendered. Stephen Gaston became a prisoner of war.

FORCED TO LIE

J. Walter Elliott, a twenty-eight-year-old lawyer "with a brick-red beard," joined the Tenth Indiana Volunteer Infantry in 1861, a week after Abraham Lincoln's proclamation called for troops. By July of 1864, he'd been transferred and promoted to the rank of captain in the Forty-Fourth Regiment, United States Colored Troops. (During the Civil War, the commanding officers of most African-American regiments were white.)

In October, rebel forces captured Elliott, but he was paroled and released. Immediately after his release, he rejoined the remainder of the Forty-Fourth Regiment. About 350 captured African-American soldiers from the Forty-Fourth were not so lucky. They were marched to a prison camp in Mississippi, where about 250 of them were "delivered to their former masters, or men who claimed to own them," thus returning them to slavery.

On December 2, 1864, Elliott was recaptured when he tried to steal through Confederate lines at Nashville, Tennessee. At that point, he had to protect his identity. The Confederate Congress had approved an act stating "that every white person, being a commissioned officer, or acting as such, who, during the present war, shall command negroes or mulattoes in arms against the Confederate States . . . shall be deemed as inciting [slaves to] insurrection, and shall, if cap-

To hide his identity and regiment affiliation, J. Walter Elliott gave a false name to his captors.

tured, be put to death, or be otherwise punished at the discretion of the court." Elliott didn't want his captors to know that he commanded an African-American regiment, because that would eliminate any hope of being released and returning to his men. Instead of giving them his name, Elliott assumed the identity of his cousin, Captain David Elliott, who was serving many miles away with the Union army in Georgia. "Never until I had shaken the dust of the confederacy from my feet did I disclose my identity to friend or foe," Elliott later confessed. This time, Elliott was not released from prison.

John Clark Ely kept a wartime diary that described his life as a soldier.

A FAMILY MAN

John Clark Ely was a family man and a teacher from Ohio. When he enrolled in the 115th Ohio Volunteer Infantry in 1862, he said good-bye to Julia — his wife and his "hearts choicest treasure"— and their three young children. On June 1, 1864, he opened the black leather flap of his new pocket-size diary and wrote, "Today I commence this book, today sent home the one used this past year ending with last night. Sent it with a letter to Julia, hope it may reach her safe."

Ely filled his diary with information about army life. He listed the names of sick comrades and wrote complimentary lines when a deserving soldier received a promotion. He noted the capture of rebel soldiers.

In 1864, Ely's company was stationed in small, single-building forts called blockhouses near Murfreesboro, Tennessee. Their orders were to protect the tracks of the Nashville and Chattanooga

Railroad from destruction by Confederate forces so that trains could continue to deliver supplies to the troops.

As a sergeant, Ely had numerous important duties. He carried muster rolls and reports from officers in one city to those in another. A muster roll was the official list of officers and men in the company. Sometimes he fetched hay for the mules and horses, occasionally leading them to a field so they could eat grass. He traveled into towns, where he obtained clothing and food for his comrades.

On November 8, 1864, he served as a member of the board of election for two of the 115th's companies, counting the men's votes in the presidential election. When he heard that Abraham Lincoln had defeated George McClellan by a vote of 90 to 4, he gleefully wrote "Bully for old Abe" in his diary.

When Ely had free time, he read books or picked berries. Both pastimes offered a pleasant break from army life. He considered the purple mulberries and juicy blackberries that he picked extremely fine and very tasty.

But John Ely missed his wife, his children, and his brothers and sisters. "No letters yesterday, it seems sad and lonely to have an entire week roll by without any letters from those at home who are most dear to me." He welcomed a box from Julia that was filled with socks, suspenders, and a cake of maple sugar. But word that his four-year-old daughter was unwell and feeling very poorly worried him greatly.

Army life wasn't easy. Ely wrote that Tennessee's "very hot, hot, hot!" weather — as high as 106° F in the shade — often left him with severe headaches that lasted for hours. At times he suffered from

In 1864, the 115th Ohio Volunteer Infantry guarded a blockhouse like this one, which was near Chattanooga, Tennessee.

extended bouts of diarrhea, a complaint that frequently sickened Union and Confederate soldiers.

In early December 1864, the war closed in on the area near Ely's encampment. Slowly, General Forrest's troops gained ground on the fort where the 115th Ohio was stationed. On December 5, Ely watched as a large force of Confederate soldiers came into sight. Surrender was the regiment's only choice. Ely and fifty-nine men from his company became prisoners of war. The next day, Ely wrote a letter to Julia and informed her that he'd been captured.

AN INCREASING PROBLEM

During the first two years of the war, incarcerating great numbers of prisoners of war wasn't an overwhelming problem. Soldiers—Michael Dougherty, for example—were exchanged equally and quickly released. Then, in 1863, the exchange system began crumbling, partly because the Confederacy refused to consider a black Union soldier the equal of a white soldier in an exchange.

A second problem with the exchange program was that it returned paroled prisoners to their units, where they would continue fighting against those who had held them prisoner in the first place. In 1864, Union general Ulysses S. Grant wanted all prisoner exchanges stopped. "It is hard on our men held in Southern prisons not to exchange them, but it is humanity to those left in the ranks to fight our battles. Every [Confederate prisoner] we hold, when released on parole, or otherwise, becomes an active solider against us at once." On August 19, he advised the U.S. secretary of state, "We ought not to make a single exchange nor release a [Confederate] prisoner on any pretext whatever until the war closes. We have got to fight until the military power of the South is exhausted, and if we release or exchange prisoners captured it simply becomes a war of extermination."

As the war dragged on, the ever-increasing number of captured soldiers resulted in overcrowded prison camps in the North and in the South. Lack of food, clothing, and medicine led to starvation and disease. Conditions in the camps worsened as supplies dwindled. Sanitation was nonexistent. Prisoners died at unconscionable rates. At Camp Douglas, in Illinois, more than four thousand Confederate prisoners died during the three years between 1862 and 1865. In only fourteen months, nearly thirteen thousand Union prisoners died in a prison camp in Georgia.

CHAPTER 3

DENS OF DEATH

BELLE ISLAND and Libby Prisons in Virginia were bursting at the seams as the end of 1863 approached. The Confederacy desperately needed a new camp for captured Union soldiers. Andersonville, a town in southwestern Georgia so small that travelers were likely to miss it if they blinked as their train passed through, was the top candidate. The isolated area, unreachable from Virginia by direct rail, was out of the range of rescue raids by Union troops. Plenty of timber for construction grew in nearby forests, and open land—with access to water—was available for lease. The Confederate government's agent quickly made a deal.

"A HELL OF TORTURE AND MISERY"

Villagers refused to build a prison camp with such close proximity to their town. Undaunted, the army moved ahead, using slaves to fell hundreds of pine trees. They set the logs upright side by side into

the ground, forming fifteen-foot-high stockade walls. The finished enclosure measured 1,620 feet long and 779 feet wide. (For comparison, a football field is 300 feet long and 160 feet wide.) Camp Sumter Prison, which quickly became known as Andersonville after the name of the town where it was located, was designed to hold a maximum of ten thousand men. Prisoners started arriving in February 1864.

To prevent escape, three rows of stockade fences surrounded Andersonville Prison. The water in the stream that flowed through the center of the prison camp was often filthy, sometimes containing human waste.

Since his capture four months earlier, Michael Dougherty and 122 others from his Pennsylvania regiment had been shuffled in and out of at least three prison camps. In mid-February 1864, after a string of train rides south from Virginia, sixty men, including Dougherty, were packed into a train car for the final leg of their journey. Dougherty wished they would arrive at Andersonville, "for I am tired of being in these old freight cars for the last four or five days." He changed his mind when they "neared the wall of great square logs, and massive wooden gates, that were to shut out hope and life from nearly all of us forever."

There was no shelter for prisoners — no buildings or even tents. Dougherty and three of his comrades created a makeshift tent by combining two blankets. The men huddled together at night, their remaining blanket covering all of them as best it could. Many men didn't even have blankets; they slept lying tight against one another, relying on the body heat of the men beside them for warmth. Some prisoners dug holes in the ground and crawled inside to shelter and protect themselves from the cold. Dougherty was appalled when "one of the prisoners smothered to death . . . his hole in the ground . . . [having] caved in on him." After a week in camp, Dougherty had determined, "There is scarcely a pair of shoes in the whole place, prisoners all in their bare feet."

Andersonville Prison was foul. A stream divided the prison camp in half, east to west. "The rebels wash their clothing and themselves in this stream, horses and mules are driven into it to drink. [B]uckets, tubs and kettles belonging to the rebel camp and cook houses are washed here, and all the filth of the camps thrown

Prisoners at Andersonville made tents by stitching blankets together. The men in the foreground are washing in the stream.

into it; and then it runs through to us. We have to use it, although it is literally alive with vermin and filth of all kinds." The water disgusted Dougherty, but unless he collected rainwater or dug a shallow well in the clay-filled soil, he had no other option.

Everyone itched. "There are millions and millions of all kinds of vermin here, flies, bugs, maggots and lice, some of them as large as spiders. If they once get the best of you, you are a goner," Dougherty declared. Small gray insects called lice, often referred to as graybacks, were the blood-sucking scourge of soldiers in both armies.

("Gray-backs" was also a derogatory term that Union soldiers used for Confederate soldiers, who wore gray uniforms.) Female lice laid eggs, hundreds of them, in the seams of clothing and on strands of hair. It wasn't long before a soldier's body crawled with lice and itched from hundreds of tiny red bites. Everyone scratched. Picking lice from oneself or one's comrades was a frequent activity. Dougherty wryly noted that some days, the only reason he wrote in his diary was that "I must do something to pass away the time, beside catching gray-backs."

Union prisoners waiting near Andersonville's front gate to receive meager rations

Daily food rations consisted of a small amount of cornmeal—a cupful (or less)—and three to six ounces of raw beef or bacon (when available). If a prisoner didn't want to eat his rations raw, he foraged for dry roots to burn or he had to buy the wood from one of the prisoners who had firewood. One civilian from the town of Andersonville was authorized to sell groceries inside the camp. If a prisoner had money, he could buy vegetables and other food items from him. A family could send money to an imprisoned relative. But unscrupulous guards, and even other prisoners, sometimes stole it before it reached the intended recipient. "One Irish potato would bring from 75 cents to $1.25—a tablespoon of coarse salt 20 to 40 cents and a handful of wood 25 cents." (Converted into equivalent twenty-first-century dollars, the cost of the potato would have been about $11; the salt $3 to $6; and the wood $3.75.) Prisoners had to pay with "good United States money," not Confederate currency. During the war, one U.S. dollar, known as a "greenback," was worth at least four Confederate dollars—and even ten times that near the end of the war.

At night, Dougherty and his friends slept in shifts, guarding one another's possessions. "There is a great deal of stealing among the prisoners, and starvation is the cause of it all," he declared. Despite shortages in food and other supplies, such as soap and medicine, shipments of new prisoners—"fresh fish," as longtime prisoners called them—continued arriving, five hundred to a thousand men at a time.

Already thin from his imprisonment in Virginia, Dougherty lost even more weight, estimating that he weighed less than one hundred pounds by March 4: "It has been eight months since I was captured. I am a mere skeleton." He felt sick and weak. His bones ached. Like his comrades, he suffered with rheumatism, diarrhea, and other ailments. Men sickened with scurvy, a disease that resulted from a deficiency in vitamin C, which caused their gums to bleed and turn black, and their teeth to fall out. Formerly healthy men starved and died "by inches," Dougherty lamented. "To fall in battle is bad enough, but to be doomed to a hell of torture and misery is worse than a thousand deaths." News that three hundred prisoners died between April 9 and 12 distressed him. But Dougherty was determined to survive. "I will keep up as long as there is a spark of life left in me."

By August, more than thirty-two thousand prisoners were crammed inside Andersonville's stockade walls—three times the camp's maximum capacity. Ill and weak, Dougherty was taken to the prison hospital at the end of the month. There, patients shared beds of straw. One morning, a week after he was hospitalized, he turned over and found that the man lying on the bed beside him was dead. By then, 100 of the 123 men from Dougherty's Pennsylvania regiment had died in Andersonville Prison.

Dougherty faithfully wrote in his diary during his imprisonment. After more than a month in the hospital, he was grateful to get "hold of a new pencil . . . mine was hardly an inch long." The last entry in his diary was on December 10, 1864: "I feel no better. My diary is full; it is too bad, but cannot get any more. Good bye all; I did not think [the war] would hold out so long when

I commenced." After surviving ten months in Andersonville, Dougherty prayed he would live to see the end of the war.

On Christmas Day, while Michael Dougherty lay in the Andersonville hospital, John Ely suffered hundreds of miles away in a small prison camp in Meridian, Mississippi, where he and the other prisoners were "hungry, dirty, sleepy, and lousy." He wondered, "Will another Christmas find us again among friends and loved ones?" News that Union troops had captured Savannah, Georgia, raised his hopes that the war would end soon and he would be paroled. While he waited, he wrote letters home to Julia. During the third week of January, Ely

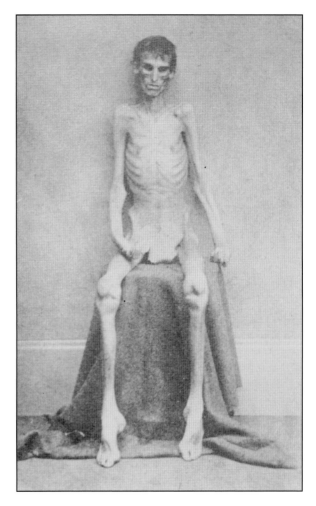

Poor conditions and rations at Andersonville led to illness and starvation. This photograph of an unidentified Union soldier held there was taken shortly after his release.

and hundreds of prisoners were removed from the prison camp in Meridian. They had no idea where they were going.

Four days later, Ely arrived at Andersonville.

Ely could scarcely comprehend the conditions in the cold, wet, prison where "men die every day" and the hospital for the Union prisoners was "like a smoke house." The only good moment was when it rained hard one night. Ely got hold of some soap and he and the men in his area "had a big time washing."

Still, Ely felt "much depressed . . . anxiety of home weighs heavy." At times anxiety gave way to anger. February 22 — George Washington's birthday — he was furious when "some scalawag opened our tent at the bottom and stole from me 1 shirt, one pair drawers [underwear], and one haversack with 4 days rations."

Heartening news of the war filtered into the prison. At the end of February, Ely wrote that General William T. Sherman, in Georgia, was "moving rapidly and capturing large numbers of [railroad] cars and provisions," and Confederate general Robert E. Lee had "evacuated Richmond and Petersburg [in Virginia]. May this prove to be true is my prayer." The news sustained Ely's spirit.

Physically, though, he struggled. Diarrhea and an upset stomach plagued him for nearly a month. Fierce pain in his back and hips made walking nearly impossible. Only continued promising news from the war front raised his hopes. The rumor that three thousand prisoners would soon be leaving the prison camp encouraged him more. But the rumor that caused the greatest excitement was that a rebel sutler — a person authorized to sell goods inside the prison — was "selling chances to leave [Andersonville] in [the] first squad." Those men would be taken to a parole camp, where they would be exchanged and either returned to service or mustered out, which meant being discharged from the army rolls and released from service.

On Friday, March 24, Ely gathered money from the men in his company—$80 in U.S. currency (about $1,200 in twenty-first-century dollars) and $80 in Confederate bills. Ely went to the sutler to buy a chance that might put him and his men among those first to leave camp. Initially, the sutler refused his offer, but when Ely added his own pocket watch, valued at $60 U.S. currency, the sutler agreed. The gamble paid off. Ely joyfully reported to his men that they had won space on the first shipment out of Andersonville.

"Peach and cherry trees all in full bloom outside" were the first things he noticed as he left the prison camp.

Walter Elliott, still maintaining the assumed identity of his cousin, had been imprisoned at another prison camp, in Alabama, but was later transferred to Andersonville, where he'd spent the winter. The news that he was among a group of prisoners to be exchanged thrilled him. "How each of us laughed and cried, shook hands with and hugged his fellows, and joining hands in a circle . . . we all joined in singing the song 'Rally Round the Flag, Boys.'"

Happy beyond words, John Ely and Walter Elliott were going home.

CAHABA

Bugler Stephen Gaston's road to prison camp did not lead to Andersonville. Instead, he was imprisoned in Alabama, in Cahaba Prison (also known as Castle Morgan in honor of Confederate general John Hunt Morgan), located where the Cahaba River joins the Alabama River. The prison's main building was a brick warehouse used for storing cotton, but with the addition of stockade walls, it was repurposed as a prison camp early in the summer of 1863. A year later, when Andersonville opened in Georgia, Cahaba Prison was temporarily closed and its prisoners transferred to the new camp.

By the time Gaston was captured, in September 1864, Andersonville was overflowing and Cahaba had reopened. Originally created to hold five hundred men, Cahaba soon held three thousand. One prisoner who survived later calculated that as horrible as conditions were in Andersonville, the overall space available for each prisoner there (thirty square feet) was five times that

During the war, a cotton warehouse near Cahaba, Alabama, was used as a prisoner-of-war camp. After the war ended, Jesse Hawes, one of the imprisoned men, drew this picture of the camp.

available to each man at Cahaba. At first, the men slept on bunks four to five tiers high made of bare, rough boards without straw or mattresses. The prisoners called the bunks "roosts," because they were stacked like the board shelves of a chicken roost and just about as comfortable. There was "lying-down room" for about six hundred men. Prisoners who arrived later slept outside on the ground.

Rations were scant and as poor as those at Andersonville, consisting of "half a pint of cornmeal, cobs, husks and all being ground together." Another prisoner noted that "once in ten days we would receive about two ounces of meat. . . . This we cut up in bits, and made porridge with our [corn]meal." In one sense, though, prisoners at Cahaba were lucky: fewer than 5 percent of the men imprisoned there died, possibly because the prison commander curbed the physical abuse of prisoners that occurred at other camps.

As 1864 drew to a close, General Sherman's Union troops fought their way across Georgia. When they captured the city of Savannah, it brought the end of the war one step closer.

By March 1865, Cahaba Prison buzzed with rumors of freedom. But the prisoners had a new problem: the Alabama River. Prisoner Ben Davis knew that the river flowed close to the prison. But he and the other prisoners made its acquaintance personally when, after several days of incessant rain in early March 1865, the river flooded Cahaba with two to three feet of water. "We had to do our cooking on rafts, and a great many men were sleeping on them," Davis stated. Prison guards floated into the camp in canoes. Prisoners stood in filthy water for nearly a week. At last, a steamboat came up the river, and camp officials ordered about six hundred prisoners transferred

On December 22, 1864, General William T. Sherman ordered that this telegram be sent to Abraham Lincoln: "To his Excellency, President Lincoln, I beg to present you as a Christmas Gift the City of Savannah with one hundred and fifty heavy guns and plenty of ammunition, and also about twenty five thousand bales of cotton."

out. According to Davis, "When the boat came in sight there was a great rush for it. Everybody wanted to get out of prison." During the following weeks, as the war's end drew near, thousands of men from Cahaba and Andersonville Prisons traveled by boat, train, and on foot to Camp Fisk, a prisoner-of-war parole camp four miles east of Vicksburg, Mississippi. At Camp Fisk, terms of exchange would be negotiated so the men could be paroled and sent north.

CAMP FISK

During March and April, a steady stream of prisoners from Andersonville and Cahaba Prisons flowed into Camp Fisk until more than five thousand men occupied the camp. U.S. Army captain George Williams was ordered to superintend the exchange of the paroled prisoners who were then encamped or arriving at Camp Fisk. But disagreements between the Confederate and Union armies regarding the terms of prisoner exchange halted the prisoners' release. In early April, Williams received orders to travel to Alabama and Illinois to meet with Confederate authorities to resolve the problems. Army captain Frederic Speed offered to assume Williams' duties while he was gone. Speed was the assistant adjutant general of the Department of Mississippi and a member of Major General Napoleon Dana's staff. His duties included keeping administrative records regarding troops and their welfare. He also assisted his superior officers in organizing the men. General Dana accepted and approved Speed's offer of help.

After the prisoners' horrific experiences at Andersonville and Cahaba, freedom was especially glorious. Even though John Ely was

Prisoners from Andersonville and Cahaba arrived at Camp Fisk by train, by boat, and on foot. At the camp, located near Vicksburg, Mississippi, they received plenty of rations and eagerly waited for news of parole.

exhausted from traveling in cramped railroad cars, marching over uneven terrain, and wading across waist-deep streams on his way to Camp Fisk, he marveled at the beauty of the world: "All along the road today were many flowers in bloom such as peach, cherry, plum, crab-apple, honey-suckle. . . . June berry, soft maple, dogwood and many little ones." He admired the rich farming country and fine stands of oak, hickory, elm, and birch trees. When he arrived at Camp Fisk, he wrote, "Oh, this is the brightest day of my life long to be remembered." John Ely was glad to be alive. Within weeks, he would see Julia and his children, including Anna, a daughter born after he enlisted. From camp, he wrote five letters to his wife and longed for one from her. "Oh, how I wish I would hear from Julia, it seems as if it would do me more good than anything else." Impatiently, he waited in camp for word that he and his company had been paroled. One of Ely's comrades from the 115th Ohio, echoed the feeling: "Our hearts leaped within us with anticipation [of soon being home]."

Stephen Gaston was among the last group of prisoners released from Cahaba. When he arrived at Camp Fisk in mid-April, he saw the American flag

On April 9, 1865, in the home of Wilmer McLean, in Appomattox, Virginia, Confederate general Robert E. Lee surrendered his army to Union general Ulysses S. Grant. Artist Alfred Waud drew this image of Lee as he rode away from the McLean house.

for the first time since his capture. "It did my very soul good to see the old flag floating in the breezes . . . proclaiming to the world that it still is able to shelter those who desire its protection." The men around him cried tears of joy. Some of them shouted. Many simply said, "Thank God."

There was food and plenty of it at Camp Fisk. When Walter Elliott arrived, he went straight to the commissary, where the soldiers' food was stored. There, barrel after barrel of pickled cabbage was rolled out for the men. He and others smashed open the tops of the barrels. And then, Elliott declared, "[We] ravenously devoured the cabbage and licked the vinegar from our fingers, the sweetest dainty to my bleeding gums that ever I tasted." After that, "We feasted on pickles." Fed ample rations during the next weeks, the men regained strength.

And then information that the men had longed to hear filtered into camp. On April 9, 1865, General Lee surrendered the Confederate army of Northern Virginia to General Grant. John Ely jubilated at the news: "Lee has caved to Grant, bully, bully, glorious bully." Rumors circulated that other Confederate generals would soon surrender. It was clear that the war's end was approaching. A new excitement filled the air at Camp Fisk. "Bully may we soon see our sweethearts," Ely exclaimed.

This form, signed by Robert E. Lee and six of his staff officers, pledged that as paroled prisoners of war, they would no longer fight for the Confederacy or take up arms against the United States.

CHAPTER 4

A LARGE AND SPLENDID STEAMER

RIVERS AND THE BOATS that navigated them played several important roles in the Civil War. The rivers, including the Mississippi, served as highways for defense, transport of soldiers, and delivery of supplies. Confederate and Union governments commandeered commercial steamboats and refitted them for their navies. By enclosing their decks and outfitting them with artillery, they became lethal gunboats. Steamboat companies often contracted with an army to transport clothing, blankets, food, ammunition, and troops. Among the troops transported were prisoners of war, who were exchanged and being shipped north to either rejoin their companies or be mustered out. Transporting troops became a lucrative business for steamboat operators.

LAUNCHING THE *SULTANA*

Nearly one-fourth of the steamboats that ran on western rivers were built in Fulton, Ohio, near Cincinnati. During 1862, employees at

On a daily basis, steamboats loaded with cargo and passengers lined the wharf in Cincinnati. Many of them were built in nearby Fulton.

the John Litherbury Boatyard, in Fulton, constructed twin side-wheel steamboats on the bank of the Ohio River. One of them was the *Luminary;* the other was the *Sultana,* owned by Captain Preston Lodwick.

Litherbury employees sawed and assembled countless pieces of lumber as they crafted an enormous wooden skeleton into the *Sultana*'s 260-foot-long and forty-two-foot-wide hull. They shaped and nailed two circular wheelhouses to cover the boat's thirty-four-foot-high paddle wheels. The seven-foot-deep hold had plenty of cargo space, yet the boat's draft was only thirty-four inches, perfectly designed for navigating on western rivers.

The *Sultana* had four decks. Its main deck, just above the water level, contained the machinery and boilers. Toward the bow, a central grand staircase ascended to the mostly enclosed cabin deck, where the main cabin and passenger staterooms were located. Several steep, narrow staircases on the cabin deck led to the third deck, a wide-open area called the hurricane deck, possibly because it was not enclosed, so passengers on it were exposed to the wind.

While under construction on the bank of the Ohio River, the Sultana *would have looked much like this boat, named the* City of Hickman.

In the central portion of the hurricane deck, a smaller raised deck, called the texas, contained a large cabin that was partitioned into small rooms to accommodate the boat's officers.

A short, steep staircase led from the texas up to the pilothouse, the *Sultana*'s command center. There, forty feet above the water, the ship's pilot had a 360-degree view of the river. A wooden pilot wheel, taller than a man, dominated the pilothouse, the lowermost portion of the wheel extending down through the floor. Hidden from view, two ropes attached to two of the lower spokes of the pilot wheel — one to a spoke on the lower left, the other to a spoke on the lower right. From the wheel, the ropes passed down through the texas and cabin decks, where they connected to the tiller, an extension of the boat's rudder. Depending on which way the pilot turned the pilot wheel, either the left or the right rope was pulled. The tiller and rudder moved in response. In this way, the pilot could steer the *Sultana*.

To prevent sparks from setting flammable cargo alight, Lodwick installed extra-tall smokestacks. The two exposed smokestacks, or chimneys, extended from the boiler area up through the cabin and hurricane decks, in front of the texas deck, and higher than the pilothouse by an additional fifteen to twenty feet. Traditionally, the wooden structure of the main and cabin decks hid the lower portion of the smokestacks from sight. But Captain Lodwick ordered the area around the *Sultana*'s chimneys left open. The open area supplied additional room for cargo, including the bales of cotton he planned to carry. More cargo meant more profit.

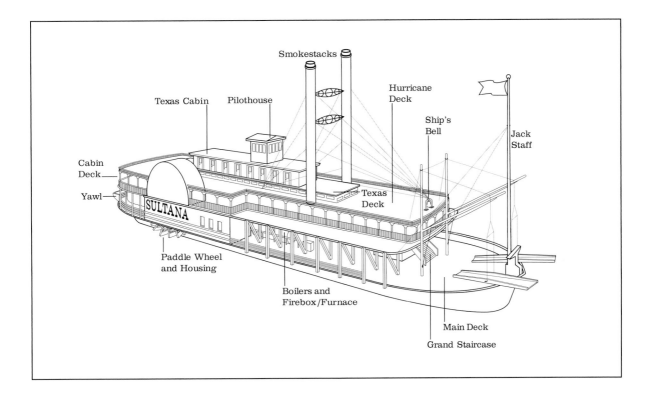

On January 3, 1863, Litherbury's boatbuilders slid the *Sultana* into the Ohio River. The *Cincinnati Daily Commercial* newspaper declared that the *Sultana* and the *Luminary* were "large and splendid steamers, designed for the New Orleans trade."

LUXURY

The *Sultana*'s steam-powered machinery was impressive, but the vessel truly became splendid when workers turned their attention to passenger needs and other finishing details. No expense was spared in constructing the *Sultana*'s "neat, tasty, capacious, and

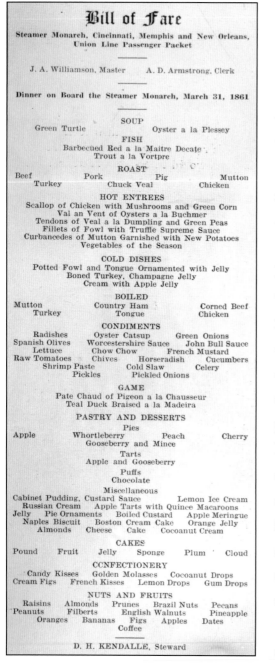

Bill of Fare

Steamer Monarch, Cincinnati, Memphis and New Orleans,
Union Line Passenger Packet

J. A. Williamson, Master   A. D. Armstrong, Clerk

Dinner on Board the Steamer Monarch, March 31, 1861

SOUP
Green Turtle   Oyster a la Plessey
FISH
Barbecued Red a la Maitre Decate
Trout a la Vortpre
ROAST
Beef   Pork   Pig   Mutton
Turkey   Chuck Veal   Chicken
HOT ENTREES
Scallop of Chicken with Mushrooms and Green Corn
Val an Vent of Oysters a la Buchmer
Tendons of Veal a la Dumpling and Green Peas
Fillets of Fowl with Truffle Supreme Sauce
Curbancedes of Mutton Garnished with New Potatoes
Vegetables of the Season
COLD DISHES
Potted Fowl and Tongue Ornamented with Jelly
Boned Turkey, Champagne Jelly
Cream with Apple Jelly
BOILED
Mutton   Country Ham   Corned Beef
Turkey   Tongue   Chicken
CONDIMENTS
Radishes   Oyster Catsup   Green Onions
Spanish Olives   Worcestershire Sauce   John Bull Sauce
Lettuce   Chow Chow   French Mustard
Raw Tomatoes   Chives   Horseradish   Cucumbers
Shrimp Paste   Cold Slaw   Celery
Pickles   Pickled Onions
GAME
Pate Chaud of Pigeon a la Chausseur
Teal Duck Braised a la Madeira
PASTRY AND DESSERTS
Pies
Apple   Peach   Cherry
Whortleberry
Gooseberry and Mince
Tarts
Apple and Gooseberry
Puffs
Chocolate
Miscellaneous
Cabinet Pudding, Custard Sauce   Lemon Ice Cream
Russian Cream   Apple Tarts with Quince Macaroons
Jelly   Pie Ornaments   Boiled Custard   Apple Meringue
Naples Biscuit   Boston Cream Cake   Orange Jelly
Almonds   Cheese   Cake   Cocoanut Cream
CAKES
Pound   Fruit   Jelly   Sponge   Plum   Cloud
CONFECTIONERY
Candy Kisses   Golden Molasses   Cocoanut Drops
Cream Figs   French Kisses   Lemon Drops   Gum Drops
NUTS AND FRUITS
Raisins   Almonds   Prunes   Brazil Nuts   Pecans
Peanuts   Filberts   English Walnuts   Pineapple
Oranges   Bananas   Figs   Apples   Dates
Coffee

D. H. KENDALLE, Steward

The Sultana's *owners prided themselves on offering a wide variety of choices on their menu, similar to the meals offered on the* Monarch, *another steamboat that traveled western rivers.*

finely furnished" long main cabin. Chandeliers hung from the ceiling in the main cabin and in the ladies' cabin, which also had fine carpet on its floor. Tablecloths, stylish glassware, and china plates adorned the tables during meals. Small stoves in the cabin ensured passengers' warmth.

Despite the overall luxury, no one had a private bathroom. There were two main restrooms, each containing a few toilets, for passengers on the cabin deck. The women's restroom was on one side of the boat, the men's on the other. They were located behind the paddle wheel housings, or covers. Human waste from the toilets dropped straight into the river, and the *Sultana*'s churning paddles "flushed" it away from the boat. A chamber pot, regularly emptied by a maid, was provided in each stateroom and in the rooms on the texas deck.

Staterooms lined both sides of the cabin, each containing two sleeping berths. The *Sultana* could accommodate seventy-six cabin passengers. It was also licensed to carry three hundred deck passengers, people who brought their own food, and ate, sat, and slept on the main deck during the voyage. Deck passengers did not have any kind of private quarters. Deck passengers and crew probably shared two restrooms on the main deck, also located behind the paddle wheel housings. The crew had its own sleeping area. Eighty to eighty-five crew members — mostly men — ran the boat or served the passengers.

White paint brightened the boat's wooden surfaces and fanciful scrollwork edged the ceilings. The name SULTANA was emblazoned in six-foot-tall black letters on each wheelhouse. Such attention to detail underscored that this was a "magnificent craft" on which passengers could "anticipate an agreeable trip." Since the *Sultana* could also hold a large amount of cargo, Captain Lodwick considered the $60,000 price tag (over $1 million today) for constructing and outfitting it as money well spent.

Last, but not least, the *Sultana* was stocked with lifesaving equipment. It had life belts for passengers, fire buckets filled with sand for smothering a shipboard fire, and a lifeboat — but only one.

The main cabin on the Sultana *probably looked much like this one, on the* City of Alton. *At mealtimes, the* Sultana's *crew set up linen-covered tables so the passengers could dine in luxury.*

STEAM POWER

The *Sultana*'s power began with its four iron boilers, which were added during the weeks after the hull was launched into the river. Each boiler was eighteen feet long with a forty-six-inch diameter, and they were installed side by side. Packed inside each boiler were twenty-four long tubes called flues. This type of boiler is called a tubular boiler.

To generate steam, the engineer pumps river water into the boilers. Firemen stoke the firebox, which is located beneath the

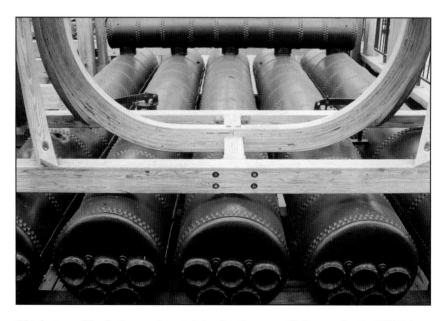

This battery of five boilers, each containing five flues, provided steam for the USS Cairo. *In comparison, the* Sultana's *battery of four boilers, similarly arranged, each contained twenty-four flues. The wooden beams represent the chimneys. A protective iron shield encased the battery.*

boilers, with coals. The flues inside the boilers fill with hot gas emitted by the burning coal and channel it the entire length of each boiler, from back to front. The gas inside the flues rapidly heats the surrounding water until it boils and becomes steam, which is used to power the vessel.

Litherbury's men connected a snaking network of pipes to conduct steam from the boilers to the *Sultana*'s two engines. One engine turned the starboard, or right, paddle wheel; the other turned the larboard, or left, paddle wheel. The engineer oversaw their operation. A speaking tube extended down from the pilot-house to the engine area. Through it the pilot communicated directly with the engineer and could request him to increase the power to a particular paddle wheel.

When the paddle wheels turned, their eleven-foot-long buckets moved the boat. Since the engines operated separately, the engineer had the option of using both the *Sultana*'s paddle wheels or just one. If one side of the boat became mired or lodged against something, the engineer could use the paddle wheel on the opposite side to swing the boat free. One wheel could spin in reverse while other spun forward, increasing her maneuverability in tight spaces.

Pipes that poked up through the hurricane deck vented spent, or used, steam from the engines. Escaping steam produced a repetitive *huff*—a sound everyone recognized as heralding a steamboat.

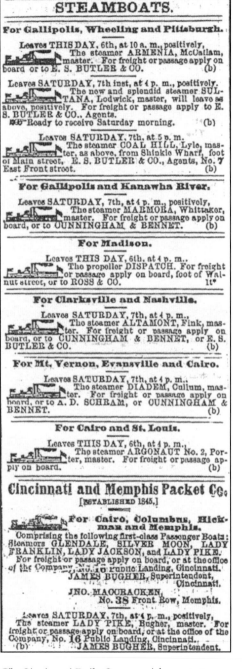

The Cincinnati Daily Commercial *newspaper regularly listed the names of arriving and departing steamboats, including "the new and splendid steamer* SULTANA*."*

In the event of a fire, a pilot was expected to ram the boat into a riverbank and let the crew and passengers run ashore.

By the first week in February 1863, the *Sultana* was ready for its maiden voyage. The boat remained in the Ohio River during February and March, where it made several runs between Cincinnati and Wheeling, Virginia (West Virginia, where Wheeling is located today, had not yet been granted statehood). But Captain Lodwick hoped it wouldn't be long before his new steamer was on the Mississippi.

ON THE MISSISSIPPI

In May 1863, the *Sultana*'s pilot navigated around the waterfalls at Louisville, Kentucky, and steered into the Mississippi River. Unfortunately, however, the war disrupted Lodwick's plans for immediate regular commercial runs to New Orleans. It was too dangerous. Confederate forces controlled the Mississippi in the vicinity of Vicksburg and prevented Union vessels from traveling freely up and down the river until July 4, 1863, when Union forces gained control of Vicksburg. Instead of steaming to New Orleans, the *Sultana* and its twin, the *Luminary*, became two of five steamboats in a convoy transporting Union troops. As the convoy neared Greenville, Mississippi, rebel forces fired on the lead boat, "wounding 12 or 14 [soldiers], some seriously." The *Sultana* was undamaged.

After Union forces gained control of the Mississippi, the *Sultana*, loaded with cotton, hay, corn, flour, and passengers, traveled to New Orleans. Twice more that summer, it came under Confederate fire. One of those times, about fifty soldiers armed with rifles raked the *Sultana* with bullets. "The upper works of the *Sultana* were somewhat riddled . . . [and] one person was injured." At summer's end, the federal government again contracted with the *Sultana*'s captain to carry four hundred furloughed Union prisoners of war upriver from Vicksburg to Cairo, Illinois.

By January 1864, the *Sultana* was a familiar visitor to cities from St. Louis to New Orleans. But Captain Lodwick's commitment to long-distance river journeys changed when he got married later that year. Even though the *Sultana* had earned him good money, he decided it was time he stayed closer to home. On March 7, 1864, he sold the *Sultana* to three Missouri men, each of whom purchased a certain number of shares in the boat. Captain James Cass Mason owned three-eighths of the boat he would soon command.

Born in Virginia, Mason came to Missouri as a child. Like Henry Shreve, he was captivated by riverboats. By the time he reached his midthirties, he was an experienced boatman and had served as an officer on two large steamboats. In 1860, he married

As shown in this image from Harper's Weekly *magazine, steamboats loaded with soldiers being shipped from one place to another became a common sight on western rivers during the Civil War, and transporting soldiers developed into a lucrative business for steamboat companies.*

Mary Rowena Dozier, the daughter of James Dozier, a wealthy Missouri steamboat captain, manufacturer, and landowner. Dozier owned several steamboats, including the *Rowena,* which bore his daughter's name. Mason became the *Rowena*'s captain and commanded it on the Missouri and Mississippi Rivers.

Mason had an excellent reputation as a boatman, but he was a businessman, too. As such, he transported cargo of all kinds. He received payment for transporting federal troops, but he also was willing to transport goods that aided the Confederacy. While the *Rowena* was on a run from St. Louis to Memphis in February 1863, officers from the Union navy boarded the boat and seized its cargo, a load of boxes labeled "dry goods." When the boxes were pried open, the officers discovered saddles, medicines in amounts deemed too plentiful for family supplies, and twenty-nine hundred pairs of pants for Confederate uniforms. The items were scheduled for delivery at places "not occupied by United States forces and infested with rebels." The navy confiscated the cargo and the boat, which was not returned to its owner.

Months later, when Mason became part owner of the *Sultana*, he already had a passing acquaintance with it—literally. They had first "met" on May 9, 1863, while Mason was the captain of the steamer *Belle Memphis*. That day, three steamboats—the *Belle Memphis*, the *Sultana*, and the *City of Alton*—left Memphis bound for Cairo and finally St. Louis. Mason, who was known as a speed demon, wasted no time. With engines stoked, Mason's boat made all of its scheduled stops, remaining at each one only long enough to unload mail, freight, and passengers and load on more. The *Belle Memphis* reached St. Louis in forty-seven hours and forty-five minutes, a blazing record that garnered rave

James Cass Mason had a reputation as a responsible steamboat captain. But he also enjoyed racing against other steamboats when they had a common destination.

reviews in the *Daily Missouri Republican*'s "River News" column on May 12, 1863. Even though Mason had left the *Sultana* in the *Belle Memphis*'s wake, he liked what he saw enough to buy the rival vessel.

As a part owner of the *Sultana,* Mason quickly resumed runs to New Orleans. By the end of April, the *Sultana* had carried 403 hogsheads, or large barrels, of sugar along with 189 men of the Sixtieth Indiana Regiment upriver from New Orleans to Cairo. The next month, on its return south, soldiers and horses of the Third Michigan Cavalry filled its decks on the trip from St. Louis to Little Rock, Arkansas.

The *Sultana* journeyed up and down the Mississippi River multiple times during the summer and autumn of 1864. In December, it yet again came under gunfire, but was not damaged. During the first three months of 1865, the *Sultana* continued its regular passenger and freight runs on the Mississippi. In April, though, Union soldiers would again fill its decks. This time, instead of transporting them to war, the *Sultana* would bring paroled prisoners home.

CHAPTER 5

FREEDOM

ON APRIL 13, 1865, Captain Mason ordered the *Sultana* to depart from St. Louis for New Orleans. The boat's pilots, George Kayton and Henry Ingraham—both licensed, experienced rivermen—would choose its course down the Mississippi River. Their job was navigating the river's channel—every twist, turn, and sandbar—not only in daytime but also in "the middle of the inky black night." The *Sultana*'s safety depended on their knowing the locations of snags: gnarly tangles of tree roots and branches mired in the mud, which often ripped holes in steamboat hulls. Mason had worked with Kayton for more than four years; he had confidence in both pilots.

The Sultana *was one of the many boats that regularly stopped at the St. Louis wharf.*

FORM C.

ENROLLMENT.

Enrollment in conformity to an Act of the CONGRESS OF THE UNITED STATES OF AMERICA, entitled "An Act for enrolling and licensing Ships or Vessels, to be employed in the Coasting Trade and Fisheries, and for regulating the same," approved February 18, 1793, and of "An Act to regulate the admeasurement of Tonnage of Ships and Vessels of the United States," approved May 6, 1864.

James C. Mason, of St. Louis. Mo. having taken or subscribed the oath required by the said Act and having sworn that he is owner of one Eighth of the Steamer herein named, H. A. Throckly of same place owns one fourth and Logan C. Dameron of same place owns three eighths, and that all are

citizens of the United States, sole owner of the Ship or Vessel called the **Sultana of St. Louis** whereof James C. Mason is at present Master, and as he hath sworn is a citizen of the United States, and that the said Ship or Vessel was built at Cincinnati Ohio in the year 1863. as appears by her Certificate of Enrollment No 17. issued at this office the 4th March 1864 now surrendered Change of owners &c. And the deputy Surveyor of this Port having certified that the said Ship or Vessel has one Deck and two Mast and that her length is 260 /100 feet, her breadth 41 /100 feet, her depth 6 /100 feet, her height 7/100 feet, that she measures Five hundred & Seventy eight Tons and twenty two hundredths, viz:

	Tonnage.	1/100
Capacity under tonnage deck	571	22
Capacity between decks above tonnage deck		
Capacity of enclosures on the upper deck		
Total tonnage	578	22

and that she is a Steamer has transom Stern flush on deck and plain head, having agreed to the description and admeasurement above specified, and sufficient security having been given, according to the said Acts, the said Steamer has been duly enrolled at the Port of St. Louis, Missouri.

Given under my Hand and Seal of Office at the PORT OF ST. LOUIS, this 2nd day of March in the year one thousand eight hundred and sixty five.

As required by law, Captain Mason and the other owners enrolled the Sultana for riverboat trade. The document contains a description of the boat.

On the *Sultana*'s two previous trips up the Mississippi, there had been some trouble with its boilers, but they'd been repaired at Vicksburg and again at Natchez. Nathan Wintringer, the *Sultana*'s chief engineer, was satisfied that they were okay. Still, he and the second engineer, Samuel Clemens (no relation to the author), watched them closely. Ensuring the safety of the boilers was their job.

A NATION MOURNS

The evening of April 14, the *Sultana* lay in port at Cairo, Illinois. Mason planned for a morning departure. Far away, in Washington, D.C., President Abraham Lincoln and his wife, Mary, sat inside Ford's Theatre, in special box seats reserved for high government officials. They were entertained by a comedy called *Our American Cousin*. At approximately 10:15 p.m., a man armed with a gun entered the box and shot the president in the head.

Abraham Lincoln died early the next morning.

Later that day, the *Sultana* chugged away from Cairo, its flag lowered to half-mast. It was the first boat to carry the sad news downriver. At that time, small towns relied on steamboats to bring them newspapers from other towns, as well as news that was sent by telegraph to larger cities. Whenever the *Sultana* approached a town, a crewman tolled its bell every thirty seconds, a signal of mourning. Hearing the bell, people assumed that the boat was bringing news of the war. They never expected to hear that the president had been assassinated.

When the *Sultana* reached Vicksburg, news of the assassination spread from the town to Camp Fisk. An orderly walked up and

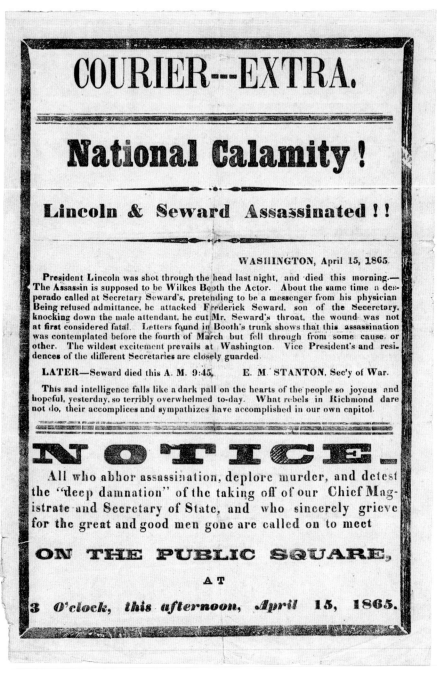

News of President Lincoln's assassination stunned the country.

down the rows between tents, informing the men of Lincoln's death. Stunned, John Ely wrote in his diary, "Our president honest old Abe was shot by J. Wilkes Booth in Washington on Friday night in theater. . . . The greatest [man] of the day. . . . Our president is gone, can it be true, too true." Michael Dougherty, who had finally been released from Andersonville's hospital and had recently arrived at Camp Fisk, seconded Ely's upset in his new diary: "Our boys are furious over the sad news, saying it is a Rebel plot." The president's death cast a pall over the camp, but, distressing as the news was, rumors of imminent transfer out of Camp Fisk soon refocused the men's thoughts on homeward journeys. This time, the rumors were true.

Within hours of Lincoln's death, a manhunt for his murderer began.

While the *Sultana* was in Vicksburg, Captain Mason learned that thousands of prisoners would soon be released from Camp Fisk. He was determined that some of them would be placed on

The orderly rows of tents at Camp Fisk were a vast improvement over the prisoners' shelters at Andersonville and Cahaba Prisons. But the men looked forward to leaving Camp Fisk and heading home.

his boat. Transporting soldiers was a moneymaker for steamboat companies. Soldiers eager to return home would willingly pay any price asked. Unscrupulous steamboat officers had been taking advantage of the soldiers — until General Grant found out. He set a fare for all soldiers at $5 for each private and $10 for each officer, a rule that was adopted by the federal government. Even so, steamboat companies made a profit. The *Sultana,* operated by the Merchants' and People's Line, competed with boats in the Atlantic and Mississippi Steamship Line for government business. Mason knew that the steamboats *Olive Branch* and *Pauline Carroll,* owned by the competing line, were on their way to New Orleans and would soon return north.

Hoping to gain an advantage over the other two boats, Mason and Miles Sells, an agent for the Merchants' and People's Line, met with General Morgan Smith and Colonel Reuben Hatch. During the meeting held on board the *Sultana,* Mason quickly came to the point. There was, "he understood, a good deal of government freight and prisoners to ship." He asked Smith if the *Sultana* could pick up a load of prisoners when it returned north. Smith promised Mason that he could have some of the prisoners from Camp Fisk.

After the meeting, agent Sells hitched a ride into town in General Smith's carriage. On the way, Smith told Sells that "he would give Captain Mason a load as he came up (back)." Furthermore, Smith said, "if Hatch and Captain Speed did not . . . give [Mason] a load," Sells or Mason should let him know. It appeared that at least some of the prisoners would be sent on the *Sultana.*

HEADING NORTH

During the third week of April 1865, General Dana ordered Frederic Speed to prepare rolls, or lists, of the names of prisoners to be paroled and shipped out of Camp Fisk. Speed went to Camp Fisk, where two of the prisoners volunteered to help him create the rolls. The prisoners listed on each roll were grouped according to the state from which they came. When the rolls were ready and the men had been supplied with rations for the trip, Speed consulted with Colonel Hatch.

FRAUD, GREED, AND CLOUT

Colonel Reuben Hatch, newly appointed as the chief quartermaster for the United States Army's Department of Mississippi, arrived in Vicksburg in February 1865. Formerly, he had been the assistant quartermaster at Cairo. As assistant quartermaster, Hatch's duties included arranging transportation for Ulysses Grant's troops and supplying them with the materials—food, fuel, lumber—they needed for carrying out military assignments. When he arrived in Vicksburg, a dark cloud hovered over his reputation.

In 1862, Hatch had been arrested for the fraudulent invoicing of army purchases—lumber and grain—to gain personal profit. He blamed his assistant. Yet another charge alleged that Hatch had "chartered the steamboat *Keystone* for the government for $1,200 per month but had reported to the government a fee of $1,800." Hatch was accused of keeping the difference.

Hatch's brother Ozias had many influential friends, including Abraham Lincoln. Ozias Hatch sent President Lincoln a letter that declared the charges against Reuben Hatch were "frivolous and without the shadow of foundation in fact." Lincoln requested that a civilian commission—not the army—investigate. Lincoln's handpicked committee acquitted Hatch of all blame. He resumed duty in February 1863.

Washington D. C. 31. Jan 1862

To The President of the United States

On behalf of Captain Reuben B. Hatch Quarter Master at Cairo Illinois I respectfully ask that under the Articles of War (see Article 92) You order a Court of inquiry into the official Conduct of Captain Hatch.

A Court Martial has been ordered on one charge, but others have been insinuated and I respectfully ask you to call a Court of inquiry under the Article of War above referred to as speedily as the good of the service will permit.

Very Respectfully
Your Obedient servant
Jackson Grimshaw
Quincy Illinois

This note, written by Jackson Grimshaw, a lawyer from Illinois, officially requested that Abraham Lincoln order a court of inquiry, a tribunal that investigates military matters, into Reuben Hatch's conduct as assistant quartermaster.

Still, personal and legal troubles dogged Hatch. He resigned from the army multiple times, but each time he withdrew the resignation. Again, his brother interceded. At Ozias Hatch's request, President Lincoln wrote to secretary of war Edwin Stanton, asking that Reuben Hatch be promoted. In his letter, Lincoln stated that "O[zias] M. Hatch, whom I would like to oblige, wants Capt. R. B. Hatch made a Q[uarter]M[aster] in the Regular Army— I know not whether it can be done conveniently, but if it can, I would like it."

On February 1, 1865, a military examining board questioned Reuben Hatch. The board concluded that "Hatch was mentally unqualified to be an assistant quartermaster" and further stated that "of the 60 officers who have appeared before this board not more than 1 or 2 can compare with Capt. Hatch in degree of deficiency . . . he is totally unfit to discharge the duties of assistant quartermaster." Official approval of the board's report was delayed until June 1865.

Despite the board's conclusion, on February 11, 1865, Reuben Hatch was appointed chief quartermaster of the Department of Mississippi. He was ordered to report to Major General Dana in Vicksburg for duty. This assignment placed him in charge of arranging transportation and supplies for the prisoners at Camp Fisk.

A train would transport the prisoners from Camp Fisk to Vicksburg; from there, steamboats would carry them north to Cairo, where they would take another train to Camp Chase, a Union military camp near Columbus, Ohio. There the parolees would be mustered out of the army and sent home or directed to report elsewhere. General Dana estimated about one thousand men would travel per steamboat load. With the soldiers who were listed on a specific roll gathered at hand, Frederic Speed or an assistant called off each man's name. As the man came forward to board the train, his name was marked with a check. During the time army captain George Williams was in Alabama and Illinois, Speed sent north two steamboats loaded with prisoners. One of the boats, the steamer *Henry Ames,* departed Vicksburg on April 22 with slightly more than thirteen hundred prisoners.

The second steamboat, the *Olive Branch,* arrived in Vicksburg hard on the heels of the *Henry Ames*'s departure in the middle of the night. When the *Olive Branch* left Vicksburg on April 23, Speed's temper was hotter than the water in the steamer's boilers. He had not learned that the *Olive Branch* was at the levee until nine o'clock that very morning. Consequently, he could only prepare the rolls for about seven hundred men. The boat could have accommodated several hundred more.

After the *Olive Branch* departed, Speed stormed into General Dana's office and demanded that army captain William Kerns, the assistant quartermaster in charge of river transportation for the Department of Mississippi, be arrested. He told Dana that Kerns had not reported to him that the *Olive Branch* had arrived during

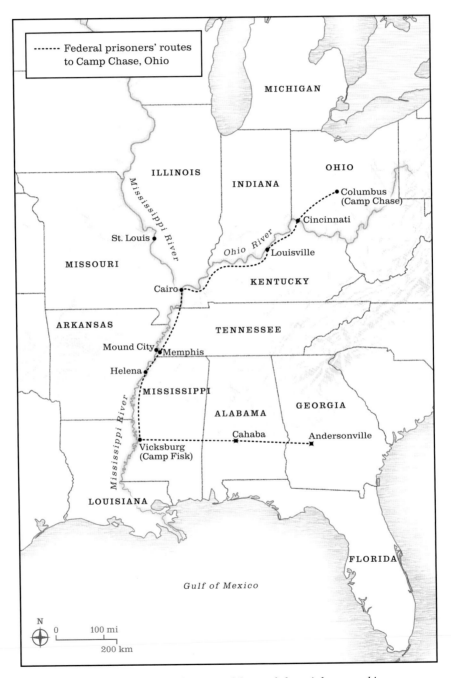

Getting to Vicksburg was only the first part of the paroled men's homeward journey.
A long boat ride up the Mississippi still lay ahead.

the night. Speed said if Kerns had reported its arrival, as he should have, there would have been plenty of time to prepare more rolls. Furthermore, Speed told Dana, Reuben Hatch had said that he learned of the *Olive Branch*'s arrival only that morning, too. (Kerns later testified that he had informed Reuben Hatch of the boat's arrival the night before.) Even worse, Speed asserted, Hatch suggested that Kerns, who was his subordinate in the Quartermaster's Department, had been bribed to keep prisoners from going on board the *Olive Branch* — paid to hold them longer, presumably in wait for a specific boat. That these unscrupulous tactics delayed a prisoner's journey home infuriated Speed. General Dana told Speed that he would not arrest Kerns until the matter could be investigated.

On April 19, while rumors in Vicksburg suggested that the first load of prisoners would soon leave Camp Fisk, the *Sultana* docked in New Orleans. Hoping for a quick turnaround, Mason champed at the bit as a last-minute appeal for additional freight delayed the *Sultana*'s departure for the return trip to Vicksburg. He knew that if he wanted to get his load of prisoners, he had to move fast — and Vicksburg was 392 miles away.

Friday morning, April 21, sixty to seventy mules and horses no longer needed by the army clomped aboard the *Sultana*'s main deck. Men corralled them in the boat's stern. Then they loaded the hold with almost 250 hundred hogsheads of sugar — about three hundred thousand pounds.

The morning wore on. Members of the Chicago Opera Troupe, a group of performers who sang, danced, and performed skits, toted instruments up one of the *Sultana*'s two four-foot-wide gangplanks.

Steamboats were periodically inspected to verify that they were being properly maintained. On April 12, 1865, in St. Louis, the Sultana was certified as meeting the legal requirements for safe operation.

Samuel Spikes tramped onto the *Sultana*'s main deck, keeping a tight hold on his valise. It held $17,000 in gold, his family's start-up money for a new life upriver. He wanted the gold stashed in a secure place, such as the *Sultana*'s safe. Elethia, his wife, counted family members—three sons, three daughters, and her niece—making sure all seven were on board. She had tucked one of her treasured possessions, the family Bible, in among her belongings. Fourteen-year-old DeWitt Spikes and his seventeen-year-old sister, Susan, climbed the staircase to the cabin deck and unpacked their belongings.

The Mississippi River's levee in New Orleans bustled with steamboat activity. On April 21, men loaded the Sultana *with horses and hogsheads filled with sugar.*

Illinoisan Daniel McLeod, looking forward to the trip to St. Louis, moved slowly up the gangplank, his gait uneven. Three years earlier, during the Battle of Shiloh, a musket bullet had shattered his right knee. He'd had to wrap a tourniquet around his leg to stanch the bleeding from the compound fracture. The doctors recommended amputation, but McLeod had refused. In and out of hospitals for the next two years, McLeod was discharged from the army in June 1864. His right knee didn't bend properly and the leg couldn't bear weight, but at least he still had it.

Seth Hardin Jr. and his wife, Hannah, thought the *Sultana* would be a fast, comfortable way to return to Chicago. Married in December 1864, the couple were on their way home from a wedding tour. After Hardin had mustered out of the Fifty-Third Illinois Infantry, he became a banker. It was time for him to get back to work; Hannah would be busy setting up their home. A porter hauled their trunk on board; Hardin carried several thousand dollars in a valise.

That afternoon, the *Sultana*'s deckhands raised the gangplanks and prepared to leave New Orleans. With a blast of its steam whistle, the boat huffed away from the wharf and into the open river. Eighty to eighty-five crew members manned their posts, either operating the boat or attending to passenger needs. About forty passengers settled in for the ride. Legally, the boat's capacity was 376 people. At only half that, everyone anticipated a relaxing trip with plenty of room for all, including a large pet alligator that the boatmen kept in a crate inside one of the wheelhouses. The gator was a curiosity that thrilled passengers — especially children.

CHAPTER 6

COUNTDOWN TO DISASTER

DESPITE VICKSBURG'S clear skies on Sunday, April 23, Nathan Wintringer, the *Sultana*'s chief engineer, was worried. For some twelve hours, as the boat had cruised toward Vicksburg, one of its boilers had been leaking. The iron in the area surrounding the leak bulged outward. Wintringer was especially frustrated because a steamboat inspector in St. Louis had given the boat a clean bill of health on April 12. He discussed the leak with Captain Mason and said he wouldn't leave Vicksburg until the boiler was fixed.

Immediately upon arrival in Vicksburg, Wintringer sought R. G. Taylor, an experienced boilermaker. Despite the late hour — nearly 9 p.m. — Taylor accompanied Wintringer to the boat. He took one look at the bulge in the boiler and said, "Why did you not have this repaired at New Orleans?" "She did not leak when the boat left," Wintringer replied. The two men disagreed about the extent of repairs. Taylor favored a large repair that required replacing a couple of the boiler's riveted iron sheets and hammering out the bulge. Wintringer suggested only a patch. When their disagreement

The wharf at Vicksburg was the departure point for soldiers from Camp Fisk.

escalated, Taylor stormed off the *Sultana*. Placated and persuaded back by Wintringer, Taylor finally agreed to patch the boiler, a temporary fix that would allow the *Sultana* to depart Vicksburg—something Captain Mason insisted they do as soon as possible, since a long delay would result in prisoners being loaded onto another boat. But Taylor cautioned Wintringer to closely monitor the water level in the boiler. If the boiler overheated, the repair might be compromised. Taylor began the twenty-hour-long repair job, but he wasn't happy about it.

GIVE ME PRISONERS!

While Taylor hammered at the boiler, Captain Mason pursued getting prisoners for the *Sultana*. First, Mason and agent Sells went to Reuben Hatch's quarters, where Mason reminded Hatch of the promise General Smith had made a week or so earlier, when they'd met on board the *Sultana*. It was now back in Vicksburg and ready to board prisoners. Did Hatch have any ready? Hatch told Mason and Sells that he'd spoken to Frederic Speed and that Speed had three hundred to five hundred men who would be ready to go in two days, on April 25. Both the number of men and the departure date displeased Mason, who wanted to leave the next day. Disgruntled, Mason told Hatch that "it would hardly pay him to wait until [the twenty-fifth] for that number of men." He further claimed that because the *Sultana* belonged to the Merchants' and People's Line, which contracted with the government, he was entitled to any of the men who were ready to go. Hatch replied that "he would give [Mason] all the men that Captain Speed could get ready; that he [Hatch] had the railroad facilities for bringing in the men [to the wharf]." If Mason needed a more specific number, Hatch said, he'd have to talk to Speed.

Downtown Vicksburg as it looked during the Civil War. Captains Speed and Williams were headquartered in the city in April 1865.

Mason and Sells next visited the boardinghouse where Speed lived, interrupting him while he ate his supper. Speed confirmed that he could prepare the rolls for three to four hundred men only — maybe not even that many — by the next day. But, Speed offered, if Mason wanted to wait a day, "he could have all the men that could be got ready to go," perhaps five to seven hundred men. Mason and Sells left, but Mason didn't intend to let the matter rest.

Finally, he went to General Smith's headquarters and bumped into George Williams, who had just returned from Illinois, where he had been resolving yet more issues concerning prisoner parole. The two men had met once before, when Williams had traveled on the *Sultana*. Mason didn't hesitate to exploit the acquaintance.

Before Speed had time to finish his tea, he received a summons to report to General Smith's office. There, Mason and George Williams further pressed Speed about sending men on the *Sultana*. Williams said he was anxious to have the matter settled. Speed reiterated that he had the rolls ready for only three to four hundred men. They decided that those prisoners would go.

As the men left Smith's office, Williams offered a suggestion. Rather than create the rolls by writing down the names of the men as they were ready and then calling each man by name to board the train to Vicksburg's wharf, as was done with previous shipments, Speed could instead use the parole camp's books and simply check off a man's name as he boarded the *Sultana*. Speed could later transfer the checked names onto different paper, thus creating rolls after the fact. Speed resisted, but he finally agreed that it could be done. In this way, all the prisoners who remained at Camp Fisk could be quickly shuttled to and loaded onto the *Sultana*. At the time, Speed believed this to be thirteen to fourteen hundred men.

Between six and seven o'clock on the morning of April 24, Chief Quartermaster Hatch visited Speed's room and asked him about the shipment of the prisoners. Hatch left knowing that all the paroled prisoners would be forwarded that day.

Shortly afterward, Speed signed and dispatched Special Orders No. 140. It stated that all prisoners of war from Virginia, Tennessee, Kentucky, Ohio, Indiana, and Michigan had been paroled. It directed that each man be provided with seven days' worth of rations and that "the Quartermaster's Department will furnish transportation." Even though it was not regular practice, Speed sent a copy of the orders to Captain Mason. Maybe it would stop him from further complaints. And so it was official: the remaining men at Camp Fisk were finally going home.

BOARDING THE *SULTANA*

With the orders issued, Speed and Williams rode the train to Camp Fisk. On the way, they talked about transferring the men out of camp. Williams agreed that Speed should continue to supervise the exchange, since Speed was familiar with the process.

Williams had already ordered Lieutenant Edwin Davenport to go to Camp Fisk to assist Speed. With Davenport's help, the men organized themselves into groups by state. As soon as the train arrived at Fisk, a crush of prisoners pressed forward to get on board. Davenport, Speed, and Williams began loading prisoners onto the train.

The first trainload, carrying 800 to 850 soldiers, left Fisk around noon. Williams accompanied the men and told Speed that he would count the men as they boarded the *Sultana* from the wharf boat. (In lieu of using a permanent dock, most towns along western rivers anchored an old boat, called a wharf boat, to the riverbank to serve as a floating dock. To load and unload, steamboats tied up to the wharf boat.) Speed watched the train depart and then, since it was mealtime, decided to grab something to eat.

Meanwhile, Captain William Kerns, who served under Hatch's command in the Quartermaster's Department and was in charge of river transportation, was worried. Earlier that morning, Captain Mason had visited Kern's office and told him that the *Sultana*'s boiler repair would soon be finished, that the boat was ready to take on a shipment of prisoners, and that he intended to leave Vicksburg at about six o'clock that evening. Kerns had received orders that all the men from Camp Fisk, plus those who were in the Vicksburg hospitals, would be going north together. Concerned that there might be too many men for one boat, he suggested to Hatch that some of the men be placed on the steamer *Lady Gay,* which was docked beside the *Sultana*. Hatch said it wasn't up to him and that he had nothing to do with transferring the men. Instead, Hatch contacted Speed, who, believing the shipment would only be about fourteen hundred men, replied to Kerns that all the men could go on the *Sultana*. Kerns released the *Lady Gay* for departure. Its decks were empty.

At the wharf, George Williams stood at the gangplank and counted the first trainload of men as they boarded the wharf boat.

After the last man passed, Williams considered his job done and went to his office in town. Williams did not return to the *Sultana* until evening.

Meanwhile, the men from the first trainload settled on the *Sultana*'s main deck. Then a group of about three hundred soldiers who had been under treatment in Vicksburg's hospitals walked down to the wharf and boarded the boat. Dr. George Kemble, the chief medical director of Vicksburg, made sure his patients were settled and resting comfortably, the frailest of them on cots. There were now between 1,100 and 1,150 soldiers on board, far exceeding the *Sultana*'s legal capacity of 376 passengers. But during the war, the army often shipped a thousand soldiers on the larger steamboats. While the army took a steamboat's legal capacity into consideration, it "placed on board [as many soldiers] as could go comfortably. And the law in regard to passengers did not govern carrying troops on the Mississippi River." The soldiers filled the *Sultana,* but it was not particularly overcrowded at that point.

THE CROWDING CONTINUES

Unbeknownst to Frederic Speed, a second train arrived at Camp Fisk while he was at his noon meal. That train, loaded with about 450 men, was on its way to Vicksburg before Speed returned from lunch. The second trainload of men arrived in Vicksburg in mid-afternoon, while Williams was away from the wharf. Alarmed by the number of men on board the *Sultana* (up to 1,600 at that point), and knowing that more were still at Fisk, army captain Kerns was relieved to see the *Pauline Carroll* tie up beside the *Sultana.*

Surely some of the men could go on it. Kerns notified Hatch of the boat's arrival and told him it was empty. Hatch said that he could not detain the boat. Not content with Hatch's response, Kerns asked General Smith to intercede and place some of the men on the *Pauline Carroll.* After speaking with Smith, Kerns talked to the *Pauline Carroll's* captain. Although his boat was running late, he agreed to delay his departure to see if there was a surplus of men on the *Sultana*. Since the *Pauline Carroll* had very few people on board, the captain wouldn't mind the business.

The growing crowd on board the *Sultana* also disturbed Dr. Kemble. Knowing that overcrowding would cause discomfort to the ill men, he visited General Dana and informed him about the less-than-favorable situation. Dana told Kemble to use his own judgment. Kemble removed his patients, leaving between 1,250 and 1,300 soldiers on board.

As John Ely was waiting to board the *Sultana,* he noticed that the river was "very high over [the] country every where." Although the past few days had been fine, recent spring rains and melt-water from ice in the north had swelled the Mississippi River to flood stage. Water surrounded the barns, sheds, and houses built on the river's floodplain. In many places, it was impossible to see land at all. When Ely boarded the *Sultana,* he thought it was "a large but not very fine boat." Once on board, Ely and others from the 115th Ohio Infantry, having "stuck together through all of our afflictions during the war," chose to remain together. As they searched for a place to sit, they saw Mr. Taylor repairing the boiler. Since the main deck was already crowded, Ely and the men of the 115th climbed to the hurricane deck and settled near the boat's bell. The *Sultana*'s chimneys towered above them.

Michael Dougherty boarded the *Sultana* without any of his comrades from Pennsylvania. All 122 of them had died at Andersonville.

Late in the afternoon, George Williams returned to the wharf boat. Like Speed, he was unaware that a second shipment of men had boarded the *Sultana*. He sent a telegram to Speed at Camp Fisk telling him to hurry up and send more men. Speed, who was loading men onto a train as fast as he could, tersely replied that he'd send them when he was ready.

A third, and final, train left Camp Fisk between four and five o'clock with 800 to 850 men. Speed joined them for the ride. Only a handful of prisoners deemed too ill for the journey remained in camp. A later roll call at Fisk suggested that fifty or more ill prisoners sneaked onto the third train.

A seemingly endless line of men boarded the *Sultana*. According to one prisoner, they were loaded like "a herd of cattle." Another prisoner agreed: "We marched on the old ship and I tell you, we was as thick as bees." They weren't the only ones taken aback by the numbers. Speed still believed that only 1,600 to 1,700 men had boarded the boat. In reality, the total number of paroled prisoners transported by trains from Camp Fisk to the *Sultana* was between 2,050 and 2,150.

SUSPICIONS OF BRIBERY

Earlier in the day, when George Williams left the wharf to go to his office in town, he had stopped at General Dana's office. While counting men as they boarded the wharf boat, Williams had heard a disturbing allegation. Lieutenant William Tillinghast, an assistant in Quartermaster Hatch's department, had informed him that an agent from the Atlantic and Mississippi Steamship Line had bribed army officers to place troops on boats owned by his company. Williams further stated that Tillinghast had implied that Frederic Speed had been bribed. (In fact, Tillinghast later admitted that *he* had accepted a bribe to place an earlier shipment of prisoners on a particular boat.) At that time, Dana knew that men in the Quartermaster's Department had been accused of accepting bribes.

After listening to Williams, Dana told him that Speed had already lodged a complaint about bribery, citing army captain Kerns. Dana must not have been certain that Kerns was guilty, since he was neither investigated nor arrested. Dana appeared not to know who, if anyone, had been bribed and toward what result. Had the *Sultana*'s captain bribed someone in the Quartermaster's Department to put all of the prisoners on the *Sultana*? Or had an agent of a rival steamboat company bribed someone to divert men from the *Sultana* and put them on a boat that belonged to the company that he represented?

Dana did not think Frederic Speed had accepted a bribe. Williams accepted Dana's assurance about Speed. But later that afternoon, when Williams returned to duty at the wharf, he remained suspicious that someone in the Quartermaster's Department was acting dishonestly for personal profit.

As the final trainload of men prepared to board the *Sultana,* Kerns threaded his way through the crowd to Speed's side. "Would it not be better to put some of the men on the *Pauline Carroll*?" he asked. By then he had already appealed to Quartermaster Hatch and General Smith a second time.

"I don't know," Speed answered.

"Colonel Hatch, General Smith, and I think though I am not positive Captain Williams have been [here] and wanted it done," said Kerns, trying his best to have men transferred to the empty boat.

Recalling the conversation he'd had a week earlier during which Hatch had implied that Kerns had accepted bribes, Speed wondered if Kerns had been bribed to load men onto the *Pauline Carroll*. He answered, "Let us see about this."

Speed halted the line of men and walked across the wharf boat, where he spoke with George Williams. He told Williams that Kerns had suggested that some of the men be placed on the *Pauline Carroll*. Williams replied, "I have been on board [the *Sultana*]; there is plenty of room and they can all go comfortably."

Speed informed Kerns that all the men would go on the *Sultana*.

A merchant from Springfield, Illinois, stood near the *Pauline Carroll*, supervising as men loaded his bales of cotton on board. It was almost dark when he watched men from the final trainload shuffle aboard the *Sultana*. He overheard the prisoners grumbling about the overcrowding. He later recalled them complaining that they didn't want to be "packed on the boat like damned hogs; that there was no room for them to lie down, or place to attend the calls of nature. . . . Some person on the wharfboat, an officer I presume, ordered the men to move forward and they all went on board."

Kerns, increasingly concerned about the number of prisoners, directly approached Williams, who was counting the men from the final trainload. Williams told Kerns that he was busy. With allegations of bribery in the Quartermaster's Department fresh in his mind, he also told Kerns that he'd heard that someone representing the *Pauline Carroll* had bribed someone to get prisoners. As a result, he was determined that it would not get a single prisoner. He refused to be involved in the matter and said that Kerns could do as he chose. But Kerns did not have the authority to order prisoners onto a different boat. That responsibility belonged to Reuben Hatch.

At that point, Kerns gave up. He released the *Pauline Carroll* for departure. It steamed away with empty decks.

Meanwhile, the prisoners finished boarding the *Sultana*. Williams grabbed a yellow envelope, a pen, and some ink and jotted down the numbers for the two groups he had counted. Then someone on either the *Sultana* or the wharf boat told Williams about the load of men who had arrived on the second train and boarded while Williams was away from the wharf. Williams added that number to his total. His final tally was 1,966 paroled prisoners on board. He reported that number to Kerns. His work done, Williams headed down the gangplank. Before he left the *Sultana,* he cautioned the men to be careful about fire. If the large number of men on board bothered him, he didn't say or do anything about it.

Whenever a large group of paroled prisoners traveled on a steamboat, a military escort always accompanied them for safety. Speed assigned Captain William Friesner and twenty-one of his men from the Fifty-Eighth Ohio Infantry as the military escort for the *Sultana*'s shipment of prisoners. And so they boarded the *Sultana,* too. At that point, with the crew, prisoners, passengers, and the military escort, there were more than 2,100 people on board the boat.

Even though the *Sultana* was overcrowded, it was not overloaded by weight. Knowing this, Captain Mason welcomed additional civilian passengers aboard, especially those who paid for a stateroom. Ann and Harvey Annis and their seven-year-old daughter, Isabella, were on their way home to Wisconsin. Harvey's

Ann and Harvey Annis, accompanied by their daughter Isabella, boarded the Sultana *as they began their journey home to Wisconsin.*

three-year service in the army had ruined his health. The previous autumn, Ann had left five of their six children at home under the care of their oldest daughter and traveled to Vicksburg to nurse Harvey. In February 1865, still seriously ill, Harvey resigned his commission as lieutenant in the Fifty-First U.S. Colored Troops. Ann, already twice widowed (her first two husbands had drowned), was relieved that her husband had survived and that they were, at last, returning to Wisconsin. Ann's relief turned to fear when she saw the *Sultana*'s overcrowded decks. She felt even more uncomfortable after "the clerk or mate pointed out to my husband and myself the sagging down of the hurricane deck in spite of extra stanchions which were put in a great many places." But the soldiers "behaved very well. . . . There was no carousing or quarrelling, and only little moving about." That eased her fears.

William D. Snow, the senator-elect from Arkansas, didn't arrive on board until almost 10 p.m. Before he retired for the night, he chatted with the *Sultana*'s clerk, William Gambrel, a part owner of the *Sultana*. In reply to Snow's comment about the large number of prisoners on board, the clerk told him it was the largest number of passengers ever carried up the river. He even showed Snow the passenger list. There were "seventy cabin passengers and eighty-five hands belonging to the boat." By Gambrel's count, about 2,175 people were on the *Sultana*. (Ongoing research indicates there were closer to 2,200 paroled prisoners, 100 paying passengers, and a crew of about 80, for a total of 2,400 people on board.) Even though the load was large, Gambrel didn't anticipate any problems; he believed the boat should arrive in Cairo on schedule. As part owner of the

Sultana, Gambrel would receive some of the money paid by the government for transporting the soldiers. His tally, which included 1,966 enlisted men and 35 officers, would have been invoiced to the government for more than $10,000 ($150,000 in today's money).

ON TO MEMPHIS

According to prisoner Nicholas Karns, it was after 11 p.m. on April 24 by the time the *Sultana*'s "bell rang and the wheels began to plow. . . . As she pulled out from her moorings we cheered and shouted," Karns recalled.

The *Sultana* was beyond cramped, especially for sleeping. In the main cabin, after supper, a row of double-deck cots — to be used by prisoners who were officers — replaced most of the meal tables. The first night out, Walter Elliott had one of the cots. Then he saw a commissary sergeant from Camp Fisk. The man had been helpful with food rations and supplies, so Elliott let him have the cot in his stead. Elliott slept in a chair. Enlisted men slept outside on the decks. Those who found enough space lay on the deck. Many of the men slept sitting up. Some had blankets; some didn't. As they'd done in Andersonville and Cahaba prisons, those who had shared with those who had none. It was hard to walk on the decks without stepping on someone.

The journey from Vicksburg to Memphis would take two days. During that time, all the soldiers on board shared one stove, cooking in shifts. If they couldn't get to the stove, the men ate their food raw. And the quality of the rations supplied by the Quartermaster's Department — pickled hogs' jowls, hardtack, coffee, and sugar—incensed J. T. Farris, an agent of the Indiana Sanitary Commission and a passenger who boarded the *Sultana* in Vicksburg. The United States Sanitary Commission, a civilian-staffed forerunner of the American Red Cross, provided "housing and meals for enlisted men who were in transit between hospitals and regiments or who were awaiting transportation home following discharge from the military." While in Vicksburg, Farris and other agents of the commission had supplied the prisoners with extra food, clothing, and small comforts such as tobacco. When Farris saw the rations furnished to the prisoners on board the *Sultana,* he wondered "who pocketed the difference between the value of the pork purchased by the Government for its soldiers, and the cheap jowls furnished by a scoundrelly Quartermaster."

There were not enough toilets to meet the needs of so many passengers. The prisoners broke holes in the *Sultana*'s paddle wheel housings and urinated directly into the churning water or used chamber pots and tossed the contents overboard. Both methods were easier than making a trip across the overcrowded deck to a toilet.

The men chatted, played cards, and read as the *Sultana* churned north. William Lugenbeal was one of the prisoners who visited the alligator kept in the *Sultana*'s wheelhouse. "We would punch him with sticks to see him open his mouth, but the boatmen got tired of this and put him in the closet under the stairway." Despite discomfort and boredom, another prisoner declared, "We were on our way home and everybody was cheered by the thought."

The *Sultana* reached Helena, Arkansas, early in the morning of April 26. Mason planned only a quick stop to deliver and pick up the

Soldiers packed the decks of the Sultana. *A photographer near the wharf in the town of Helena, Arkansas, managed to take this photo during the boat's brief stop there.*

mail, so he didn't allow the men to leave the boat. But townspeople waved from shore, and a photographer set up his camera. Prisoners moved to the landward side of the *Sultana* to return the greetings and maybe get in the picture. The sudden shift of weight alarmed Captain Mason, but he couldn't control the crowd. He turned to Captain Friesner, of the military escort, for help. "Mason . . . complained . . . that the men were careening his boat by the many going to the shore side and asked me to assist him in keeping the boat in trim [even] as the boilers might explode," Friesner recalled. He loudly urged the men to move back across the decks. Pilots Kayton and Ingraham soon had the *Sultana* back under way.

Memphis was sixty-six miles upriver, and they hoped to reach its cobblestone wharf by sundown.

As soon as the *Sultana* reached Memphis, the deckhands lowered the gangplanks. Knowing the boat would be docked for a while, many of the soldiers decided to stretch their legs onshore and get some fresh air before resuming the trip north. Soldier Hugh Kinser heard Captain Mason caution the men to return to the boat soon so they wouldn't be left behind.

Kinser, James Payne, and Nicholas Karns walked to a Soldiers' Home operated by the Memphis branch of the Sanitary Commission. Its facility on the riverfront had barracks, a kitchen, and a dining hall. The men were looking for a good meal.

The Chicago Opera Troupe had several days of performances lined up in Memphis. They gathered their gear, said good-bye to the men, and left the boat.

Stephen Gaston did not head into town. He'd noticed cargo

Memphis was a regular port of call for boats traveling along the Mississippi River.

being lifted from the hold. To earn a bit of money, he helped unload the sugar. "I found a hogshead of sugar broken — as soldiers always do find," Gaston said. He and his comrade William Block filled every container they could find with sugar. They planned "to eat the sugar . . . while going up the river to our destination." Gaston and Block carried their find up to the texas deck in front of the pilothouse. They ate sugar until it was time to sleep. "Our evening dreams were sweet, for we had eaten about two pounds of sugar each," Gaston said.

For a while, Albert King helped unload sugar, but he soon tired of the task. He made his way up the streets into Memphis. Worried that the *Sultana* might leave without him, he stayed on shore only a short time.

After supper, in the main cabin, the crew set up cots for the night. Cabin passengers returned to their staterooms and prepared for bed. Ann Annis slipped a pink nightdress over Isabella's head.

Filled with a good meal, Nicholas Karns hurried back to the boat as soon as he heard the *Sultana*'s bell. He climbed outside the railing on the cabin deck, took off his shoes, hat, and shirt, and bunched them into a lumpy pillow. Just before he fell asleep, he heard deckhands raise the gangplanks. The hands placed one of the twenty- to twenty-five-foot-long gangplanks on the boat's bow. With ropes, they hoisted the other one up until it hung level with the cabin deck, not far from where Karns lay.

James Payne, who had been farther away in town, started for the riverfront when he heard the *Sultana*'s bell. Unfortunately, by the time he arrived at the wharf, the boat had already left.

When the Sultana *stopped at Memphis's cobblestone wharf, many of the prisoners grabbed the opportunity to leave the crowded boat to stretch their legs or get a quick meal in town.*

On board the *Sultana,* Michael Dougherty and John Ely settled themselves as comfortably as they could, given the cramped space.

Daniel McLeod's right leg ached. The long trip from New Orleans had tired him, but he wasn't sleepy. He sat at a round table in the front part of the main cabin, picked up a book, and started to read.

Walter Elliott, also in the main cabin, dropped his belongings on a cot that was located directly above the boilers. Before he had a chance to lie down, the commissary sergeant who'd accepted Elliott's cot the previous night arranged for him to move to a cot farther from the boilers — a much cooler place to sleep.

APRIL 27, 1865

By 1 a.m. on April 27, Captain Mason had retired to his quarters. On the way, he "was compelled to crawl around on the rail, as the deck was so crowded with men lying down that he could not find room to step, and was in consequence made the subject of several jokes." William Rowberry, the first mate, was on duty in the pilot-house in Mason's stead.

With the *Sultana*'s paddle wheels churning, George Kayton piloted the boat to a coal barge just across the river from Memphis. There, firemen loaded one thousand bushels of coal, enough to reach Cairo, where the soldiers would transfer onto different transports to complete their journeys north to Union army camps. As usual for that time of night, chief engineer Nathan Wintringer went off duty and left Samuel Clemens in charge of the machinery. Clemens pumped more river water into the boilers. Crewmen stoked the coals until a head of steam rose in the boilers. Its engines primed, the *Sultana* was ready to go.

While the *Sultana* had been refueling, James Payne attempted to make his way to the coal barge but failed. Cursing his rotten luck, he stood in a steady rain on the sand and watched the *Sultana*'s lights disappear around the river bend. By then, it was two o'clock in the morning.

CHAPTER 7

END OF THE WORLD

GEORGE KAYTON held the *Sultana* to a steady rate upriver, about nine to ten miles per hour. Since the Mississippi was at flood stage, the current was moving at about five miles an hour in the opposite direction, but Kayton didn't think that would cause a problem. Clemens, a reliable man, would call him through the speaking tube if he had any concerns. In Kayton's opinion, "Nothing more than common was in progress."

Suddenly, with a loud roar, one of the *Sultana*'s boilers burst. Within seconds, two more boilers exploded. Steam and chunks of red-hot iron blasted upward through the center of the boat. The explosive force shattered the support structures of the main and cabin decks as if they were toothpicks. Within a minute, both decks had collapsed behind the main stairway in the center of the boat. A gaping hole replaced the staterooms and cabin area located above the boilers. Surrounding the hole, the cabin deck's broken floorboards slanted toward the fireboxes left exposed after the boilers exploded. The *Sultana*'s two chimneys, robbed of their support, toppled and crashed onto the hurricane deck. Hundreds of men on the collapsed cabin and smashed hurricane decks slid toward and then dropped into the fireboxes' blazing coals.

Steam blasted through the hurricane deck as rapidly as it had ripped through the lower decks, and hurtled splintered boards through the air like spears. Three-fourths of the texas deck was obliterated. The force of the blast flung First Mate Rowberry out of the pilothouse and into the cold river, about forty feet from the boat. When he surfaced, the river "was full, a sea of heads for hundreds of yards around." Screams for help came from all directions. Mangled bodies floated in the water. Damage to the pilothouse and steering wheel left the *Sultana* at the mercy of the Mississippi.

With the floor of the pilothouse destroyed, Kayton plunged toward the boilers and was wedged tightly among fallen debris. He wriggled loose. Believing that the flames could be extinguished, Kayton urged men not to jump overboard but to remain on the wreck as long as possible. Frantically, he searched for the *Sultana*'s red sand-filled fire buckets, but the bucket racks were empty. During the journey north, the soldiers on deck had needed drinking water. To get it, they had removed the fire buckets from their racks, emptied them of sand, tied ropes to the handles, lowered them to the river, and hauled up water. As a result, the buckets were gone when Kayton looked for them. Unchecked, the flames spread. Giving up, Kayton grabbed a plank and slipped overboard. Confusion and chaos best describe the jumble of events for the next hour.

After the Sultana *exploded, orange flames lit the night sky. Hundreds of people struggled to survive in the cold water of the Mississippi River. Hundreds more died. This image, which appeared in the May 20, 1865, issue of* Harper's Weekly, *conveyed the horror to readers nationwide.*

FIRE ON THE MAIN DECK

When the boilers exploded, chunks and pieces of iron spewed across the *Sultana*'s main deck like shrapnel shot from a cannon. Steam burst from the pipes and severely scalded dozens of men, including Samuel Clemens, who landed in the river.

Cavalryman Simeon Chelf had fallen asleep on the *Sultana*'s bow, his head resting against a post. A chunk of iron flung by the explosion glanced off his head. Thinking that rebels had attacked the boat, he wrestled free of his blanket, which had protected him from falling cinders and boards. He scrambled to his feet and surveyed the horror of the wreckage. The man next to him was alive, but the soldier beyond him was dead. He witnessed a stampede of men trample the dead body of another soldier so roughly that the dead man's clothes were torn off. Choking on smoke from the spreading fire, Chelf grabbed a plank and leaped into a clear spot in the river.

Brothers Robert, John, and Henry Hamilton had settled for the night in separate areas of the boat. Robert was asleep on the main deck midway between the boilers and the stern when the explosion startled him awake. Scared that falling timbers would crush him to death, he hurried toward the stern. There, confused men and women leaped into the river. "They were leaping off into the water on top of each other—hundreds drowning together," Hamilton later exclaimed in disbelief. Returning to the center of the boat, he picked up a long, thin board and entered the wheelhouse. From there, he "climbed down on the wheel, and got off into the water without sinking." He didn't see John or Henry.

The force of the explosion left paroled prisoner Jesse Martin feeling as though someone were kneeling on his chest, choking him. He lost consciousness. "When I came to I was down on my knees by a cow, as though I had got there to milk her," he said. It felt surreal, but Martin was thankful. He was certain that if the cow had not been there to stop him, he would have slid into the wheelhouse, where the paddles, which were still turning at that time, would have dragged him underwater and drowned him.

Martin moved to an open area of the deck, where he and another man threw anything that floated into the water to help the people already in the river. They saved one large board for themselves. Crackling flames crept closer. Finally, Martin tossed the plank overboard and the two men jumped after it. When Martin surfaced, neither the plank nor the other man was in sight. Martin swam until he found another plank, then held on for his life.

Gasping for breath, Albert King and four companions rushed to the stern. He looked back toward the bow and, aghast, saw the gangplank that had been suspended alongside the cabin deck above crash down on men and crush them. The five friends tried to break off a section of the *Sultana*'s siding, but a white horse tied to the railing got in their way and prevented them. King looked away from his friends for a minute; when he turned back, they were gone. Having no other choice, King jumped as far out as he could over the crowd in the river.

FLEEING THE CABIN DECK

Inside their stateroom, Ann and Harvey Annis heard a loud clanking sound, as if pieces of iron were rattling against one another.

Harvey opened the inner stateroom door that led to the main cabin. Dense steam filled the air. He quickly shut the door, grabbed two of the large, bulky life belts provided for the *Sultana*'s passengers, and fastened one around Ann's waist. But Isabella was too small; tied its tightest around Isabella's waist, the life belt still slid down to her ankles when she moved. Harvey tied it around himself and led Ann and Isabella from the cabin toward the stern. Carrying Isabella piggyback, Harvey gripped a rope that hung from the cabin deck and lowered himself to the main deck. Ann did likewise. "As I was descending the rope a man from above jumped on me and knocked me into the hold," Ann exclaimed. A new terror seized her in the partially water-filled space: she worried that the *Sultana*'s alligator had broken free from its crate and was swimming in the hold. Harvey pulled her back to the main deck.

Just before Harvey jumped into the river with Isabella, he lifted a door from its hinges. They could use it as a raft. Ann edged forward, ready to jump, but before she could do so, a mule stepped on her and pinned her in place. By the time she reached the water, Harvey and Isabella were nowhere in sight. Ann's life belt kept slipping, so she held on to the *Sultana*'s rudder. Frightened by the fire's increasing heat and the cinders and coal sparks in the air, Ann dropped into the water. She reached out to a man — Albert King — who was treading water, and begged him for help. King caught hold of one end of a floating plank, and then extended the other end to Ann. The two floated toward the Arkansas shore.

At the sound of the explosion, Walter Elliott sat bolt upright on his cot. For an instant, he thought he was on a battlefield. In the dark, he quickly dressed and groped his way around cots and past stateroom doors. Women and children in nightclothes ran around him on what was left of the cabin deck. Men — some half-dressed and many naked — were jumping over the guardrails and into the river. As Elliott felt his way in the fire's flickering light, he reached a gaping hole in the cabin floor — the section of the cabin where his first night's cot had been. The deck was completely gone. Peering over the rim of the hole, he saw injured and dead people "heaped and piled amid the burning debris on the lower deck."

And then, behind him, a calm voice spoke.

"Captain, will you please help me?"

Elliott turned. Daniel McLeod sat quietly on a cot close to the rim of the hole. His skin was scalded. The force of the explosion had thrown him over the table and slammed him into a wall. Both of his ankles were fractured, the bones protruding through his skin. Using the suspenders from his pants, McLeod had tied an improvised tourniquet around each ankle so he wouldn't bleed to death.

"I am powerless to help you; I can't swim," Elliott confessed.

"Throw me in the river is all I ask; I shall burn to death here," McLeod replied.

With help from another man, Elliott lifted McLeod to the edge of the deck and placed him outside the guardrail. He then turned away, certain he'd condemned McLeod to drown. McLeod, however, was determined to live. He took hold of a broken chain and lowered himself into the water.

After moving McLeod, Elliott found a life belt. But when he saw a girl preparing to jump overboard, he seized hold of her arm. He then untied his life belt and handed it to a chambermaid, who tied it to the girl.

Less than ten minutes from the time of the explosion, the *Sultana*'s hull above the surface of the water had a large gap between the bow and the stern, making it appear as though the boat had been ripped in two. Fire surrounded the boilers. Southerly winds drove the flames toward the stern. Seeking refuge, many men rushed to the bow.

Less than half an hour after the explosion, the paddle wheels and their housings, which had been loosened by the explosion, tilted dangerously, ready to fall. Elliott realized that he had to get off the boat. He picked up a mattress, tossed it overboard, and jumped in after it. When he surfaced, the mattress bobbed within reach; only one person clung to it. With lungs and throat feeling as though they were on fire, Elliott and the other man kicked to distance themselves from the *Sultana*. Minutes later, the left paddle wheel and housing toppled into the water. The river's current pushed against the paddle wheel and turned the *Sultana,* causing its bow to point downstream. Shortly afterward, the right paddle wheel tumbled into the water. Waves swamped Elliott and his companion. Choking and spitting water, Elliott was surrounded by people. Some clutched the manes and tails of live horses and mules; others grasped the bodies of dead ones. People wrapped their arms around bales of hay and boxes, or any floating object that offered hope of survival. Soon, the Mississippi swept Elliott away from the burning boat and into darkness.

Smoke forced Seth and Hannah Hardin from their cabin. With no alternative in sight, they jumped into the water. Almost immediately, the current separated them.

Elethia and Samuel Spikes struggled to keep the nine members of their family together. But once they were in the river, the lack of visibility made it impossible to stay near one another.

Surrounded by chaos on the cabin deck, Nicholas Karns sprang to his feet when the boilers exploded. "Everywhere steam was escaping, women were screaming, soldiers and crew cursing and swearing, horses neighing, mules braying, splinters flying." Men near him sawed at the ropes of the gangplank that was suspended alongside the cabin deck. Karns helped them, stepping onto the gangplank just before the ropes were cut through. With a jolt, the plank and all of the men "on it crashed down onto the heads of those on the bow of the boat below." (This was the same gangplank that Albert King saw fall.) Scrambling upright, Karns and the others shoved the gangplank into the water. It sank deeply, then shot to the surface some distance away. Karns and ten or twelve others swam to it and grabbed hold.

MEANWHILE ON THE HURRICANE DECK

Simultaneously with the havoc occurring on the main and cabin decks, similar chaos overtook the hurricane deck. Prisoner Jacob Rush was near one of the wheelhouses at the time the boilers exploded. Seeing that the hurricane deck was shattered near the center of the boat, he quickly made his way toward the stern, where he planned to jump overboard. Looking down, Rush saw four or five men — deckhands, he believed — launch the *Sultana*'s yawl, a small boat that hung from the stern. He listened as a woman — the wife, he thought, of one of them — pleaded with the men to take her with them. In their hurry to escape before people floundering in the water could overtake the yawl, the men disregarded her plea and left.

Before the paddle wheels fell and the boat turned around, Rush helped launch the *Sultana*'s only lifeboat from the hurricane deck. No sooner had the lifeboat touched the water than "crowds from each deck jumped into it, striking upon one another, and the boat was capsized." The boat repeatedly turned over, "burying from fifty to seventy-five [people], who were trying to climb in from the opposite side." Few people managed to cling to the mostly submerged lifeboat as it drifted downstream. Having watched the horrific scene from the deck, Rush realized that the lifeboat had drowned dozens more people than it saved. Had he jumped overboard when the lifeboat was launched, he might have been one of them.

Responding to screams from the river, Rush hurled stateroom doors, blinds — anything he could tear loose that would float — into the water. He helped shove the gangplank off the bow. Immediately, people scrambled onto it. Rush hesitated before jumping overboard. While waiting, he saw another man ripping off doors "and throwing them off into the river to assist those in the water." He thought it was Captain Mason.

Ben Davis had awakened shortly before the explosion. Deciding that he wanted to smoke his pipe, he squeezed between soldiers on the stairs to the lower decks and went to the boilers, where he could light it. On his return to the hurricane deck, he smoked for about ten minutes. "When I got through with my smoke I got a canteen of water, and was about to take a drink when the boiler exploded, and the canteen flew out of my hand. I never saw it again. . . . I thought the boat had all gone to pieces." Davis realized he would have to jump into the river. Like Ann Annis, he was worried about the *Sultana*'s pet. "I guess everyone that was on the *Sultana* knew something about the monstrous alligator that was on the boat. . . . While the boat was burning the alligator troubled me almost as much as the fire." Despite this concern, Davis decided the river offered his best chance for survival. "There were so many people in the water you could almost walk over their heads," Davis declared. He slipped over the side into a clear space and struck out for shore.

Ann Annis and Ben Davis weren't the only people thinking about the alligator. By the time William Lugenbeal fought his way downstairs to the main deck, "every loose board, door, window and shutter was taken to swim on, and the fire was getting very hot. I thought of the box that contained the alligator." He hurried to the closet where the crew kept the alligator's crate. Bayonet in hand, Lugenbeal dragged out the crate, opened it, and killed the alligator. "I took off all my clothing except my drawers, drew the box to the end of the boat, threw it overboard and jumped after it." In the river, he climbed into the crate, his feet hanging over the end. Lugenbeal kicked away anyone who approached his makeshift boat, fearing they would swamp it.

William McFarland was jammed with others on the hurricane deck at the stern. When the boilers exploded, he thought he was dreaming. In his dream, he heard someone say, "There isn't any skin left on their bodies." He opened his eyes, horrified to realize it was no dream. "I saw the pilothouse and hundreds of [men] sink through the [cabin] roof into the flames." He dived into the river. Looking up at the boat, McFarland saw a woman holding a small child. She wrapped a life belt around the child's waist and threw him or her overboard. But the life belt slipped down, and the child bobbed to the surface upside down. Before McFarland could react, the mother sprang into the water and grabbed the child. The current swept McFarland away from them.

Even before McFarland plunged into the water, the blast had destroyed the support structures for the two smokestacks. One fell backward and slammed into the remnants of the pilothouse. The other toppled forward, where John Ely and his comrades of the 115th Ohio Infantry slept, and smashed the hurricane deck, which collapsed onto the cabin deck.

Some survivors said that immediately following the explosion they thought about how much they needed to get home to their families. Had John Ely thought of Julia and his children? No one knows. John Ely, who loved reading letters from home, was dead before dawn.

TRAPPED ON THE TEXAS DECK

When chief engineer Nathan Wintringer heard the commotion, he rushed from his quarters on the texas deck. Seeing flames, he decided to abandon the boat. He tore a shutter from a window and jumped into the river.

Stephen Gaston felt himself "raised to a height," and then he fell back onto the deck. Just a few feet away, one of the fallen smokestacks lay atop the pilothouse. Debris partially pinned him to the deck. Trapped, he used his free hand to feel beside him, where his friend William Block had been. No one was there.

Debris lay across men to Gaston's right. They begged him for help. Unable to reach them, Gaston watched helplessly as they smothered to death from smoke and the weight of debris.

Gaston, badly scraped and in pain, finally pulled himself free. Holding a cable, he swung down to the bow of the boat. Scalded people with broken arms and legs surrounded him. "Their cries made the already dark night hideous." He found an empty barrel and stripped off his clothes so they wouldn't weigh him down. Gripping the barrel tightly, Gaston jumped into the river.

Meanwhile, the *Sultana* floated downriver. People in the water had to swim out of its path or risk being hit by it. After the paddle

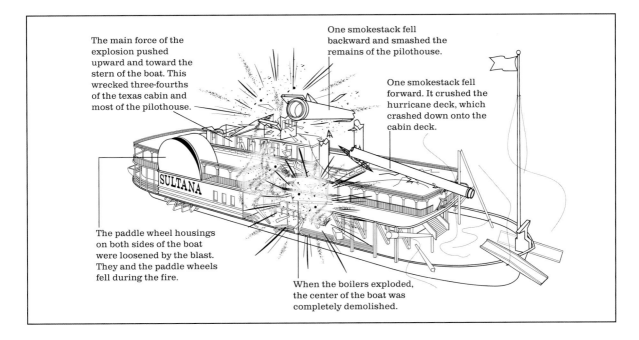

The main force of the explosion pushed upward and toward the stern of the boat. This wrecked three-fourths of the texas cabin and most of the pilothouse.

One smokestack fell backward and smashed the remains of the pilothouse.

One smokestack fell forward. It crushed the hurricane deck, which crashed down onto the cabin deck.

SULTANA

The paddle wheel housings on both sides of the boat were loosened by the blast. They and the paddle wheels fell during the fire.

When the boilers exploded, the center of the boat was completely demolished.

wheels fell and the *Sultana* turned, the wind fanned a solid sheet of flames toward the bow. Men who had earlier fled to the bow seeking refuge from flames in the stern now had to flee the bow, which by then faced south. They began jumping overboard. Within thirty minutes of the explosion, fires burned at both ends of the boat. As Nicholas Karns floated downstream, still clinging to the gangplank, he looked back at the *Sultana*. The flames seemed to touch the sky.

AN ICE-COLD PLUNGE

Everyone who jumped into the Mississippi had the same thought: get to shore. But the flooding Mississippi had erased the riverbank. In some places dry land was nearly two miles away. And finding it wasn't easy. "The glare from the burning boat upon the water blinded us so we could not see the timber along the banks," declared Hugh Kinser. Even worse, it was impossible to tell how deep the water that swirled around the trees and buildings was.

Joseph Mayes couldn't swim. Clinging to boards, he fought the current every inch of the way toward the riverbank. "Sometimes I would get within fifty yards of the shore and the current would carry me toward the other side of the river and then I would try for that side, but [the current] would strike me again; so I just kept floating back and forth across the river."

The current separated family members. It swept newlyweds Seth and Hannah Hardin apart as soon as they jumped overboard. Surrounded by darkness, Seth shouted Hannah's name again and again. She didn't answer. DeWitt Spikes, likewise separated from his family, struggled alone in the swiftly flowing river.

Drifting trees and logs were the scourge of steamboat hulls. Ironically, they became life preservers for hundreds of victims. Daniel McLeod couldn't kick with his broken ankles, but he had strong arms. He swam to a cluster of branches that poked above the water and lodged himself among them.

Simeon Chelf battled waves that slapped him in the face. He dived under one wave and rode the next as he tried to conserve strength. Chelf shared his plank with another man until they steered it into some bushes and separated. Chelf let his feet dangle. Due to the flooding, he still couldn't touch bottom. He paddled farther into the brush. "Coming to a leaning willow [tree], I threw my left arm and foot over it to rest. It held about half of my body out of water, but I got chilly in that position." Still unable to touch bottom, Chelf swam back toward the main river channel. From the darkness, a man called out to Chelf, telling him that he was securely perched on a strong, dry log. Guided by the man's voice, Chelf made his way to the log. When he reached it, his arms were so numb from the cold water that he couldn't climb onto it without help. Atop the log, Chelf rubbed his arms and legs and hit himself on the chest until his circulation improved.

Ben Davis reached a log among the willow trees on the Arkansas bank. Safely out of the water, he listened. "I could hear so [many men] groaning that I hollered to them to encourage them, telling them I was on shore. . . . They kept on coming till there were five of us on the log."

Holding tightly to a plank, Robert Hamilton drifted downstream alongside the *Sultana*'s hull. By then, the boat had burned down to the main deck. Unable to draw the attention of a passing steamboat, Hamilton noticed that about twenty men had climbed back onto the *Sultana*'s bow. He steered to the bow and joined them. But the bow was still smoldering and was starting to sink.

Hours passed while Albert King and Ann Annis floated in the dark. "All this time my lady companion was quiet except that she would occasionally say, 'For God's sake, tell me, do you think we will be saved?'" Finally, King's feet touched ground. They had reached a partially flooded island. King and Annis climbed onto a log wedged among the brush. Their combined weight sank the log until they were submerged up to their shoulders. "In a few minutes we became so chilled that we could scarcely speak." Although it was soon daylight, they remained fearful. They didn't see anyone who might rescue them.

Nicholas Karns and the men sharing the gangplank with him barely made it to the Arkansas shore. Several times the plank overturned as more men tried to climb on. Each time, Karns let go, then swam back after the gangplank righted itself. When they saw a boat coming downriver, everyone yelled, but the boat passed them by. Karns felt himself losing hope as its lights disappeared into the distance. "I was chilled to the marrow," he said. But he didn't give up.

The gangplank drifted until it lodged in the top of a fallen tree. Karns climbed into the tree. Another man had floated to the tree on a bale of hay. Unlike Karns, he had all his clothes on. The man shared his clothes with Karns, who was shivering. Then the man wrapped his arms around Karns to prevent him from falling out of the tree. Karns fell into a stupor until his comrade roused him after daylight. At that point, they broke sticks from the drift of wood, climbed back onto the gangplank, and rowed themselves to a small stable surrounded by water. Karns and his companion climbed onto its roof. "Just a little below us stood a large mule, mid-deep in water. I suppose someone had cut him loose and swam out with him. On the other side I saw a man hanging to a bush by his hands. He had bent it over and was about half suspended out of the water, without a stitch of clothing. He must have been near the boilers, as his body seemed in blisters all over."

Elsewhere in the river, William McFarland had finally managed to climb onto a log. In the dim predawn light, he saw men hanging from branches or perching on logs all around him. Some were flapping their arms to keep warm. Others sang songs to keep themselves awake in the cold water. Some were croaking like frogs. McFarland didn't really think it was funny, but he started to laugh. Once he'd started, he couldn't stop. His hysterical laughter eventually became a shout of joy: "Imagine my surprise when I observed that woman, who I had witnessed plunge into the river after her baby, sitting a-straddle of a log about twenty feet in front of me with the little one before her." Amid the horror, finding two people that he thought had surely drowned gave McFarland reason to hope.

Daylight brought an unexpected torment. "After the dawn of day mosquitoes came on us by the thousands," declared Simeon Chelf. Still, he and those clinging to the bushes nearby were alive. And hopeful that the sun's light would make it easier for rescuers to find them.

CHAPTER 8

RESCUE

AT FIRST, people who lived along the Arkansas and Tennessee shores and those traveling on other boats didn't know what had occurred. If they were close to the river, they would have seen flames, but they had no way to judge the magnitude of the disaster. It was the victims' screams that called them to action.

LOCAL HEROES

The flaming *Sultana* eventually ran aground on one of Paddy's Hen and Chickens Islands. From his property on the Arkansas riverbank, John Fogleman saw the burning steamer. He and his sons Leroy and Dallas roped together two hewn logs, each about twelve feet long, to build a crude raft. Fogleman poled the raft into the river but stopped about one hundred feet from the boat. He feared that if he went too close, the twenty-five to thirty-five men on the *Sultana*'s bow could swarm onto the raft and capsize it in a mad scramble for safety. He shouted his concern to the men standing on the bow, and they agreed on a plan. Fogleman would take six men at a time. He promised he would return until all of the men had been carried to safety. Lying on their stomachs on the raft, the rescued men paddled with their hands and feet to make the craft move faster. For the men waiting anxiously on the burning boat, flames creeping closer by the minute, each trip lasted a lifetime. They protected their skin with wet blankets and clothing and covered their mouths and noses to avoid breathing smoke.

Finally, only a handful of men — the ones most severely burned — remained. They begged not to be left behind. John, Leroy, and Dallas did not fail them. From a nearby tree, Hugh Kinser watched them retrieve men from the burning bow "until the last man was rescued." Just before the Foglemans' last load of men reached shore, the "*Sultana* went down, its hot irons sending the hissing water and steam to an immense height." Only the boat's jack staff, the tall pole that pilot George Kayton used to sight the vessel's course, remained above the water.

For hours more, the Foglemans searched for victims. They brought exhausted survivors to their home, which became a temporary hospital. Fogleman's sixteen-year-old daughter, Frances, and twelve-year-old son, Gustav, provided first aid, hot drinks, and a wood fire for the near-frozen survivors. The Fogleman family is credited with saving about one hundred lives.

Robert Hamilton and DeWitt Spikes were among those the Foglemans rescued. Sitting near the fire at the Foglemans' house shortly after sunrise, Hamilton watched as "the two men that rescued us brought ashore the bodies of two dead women, mother

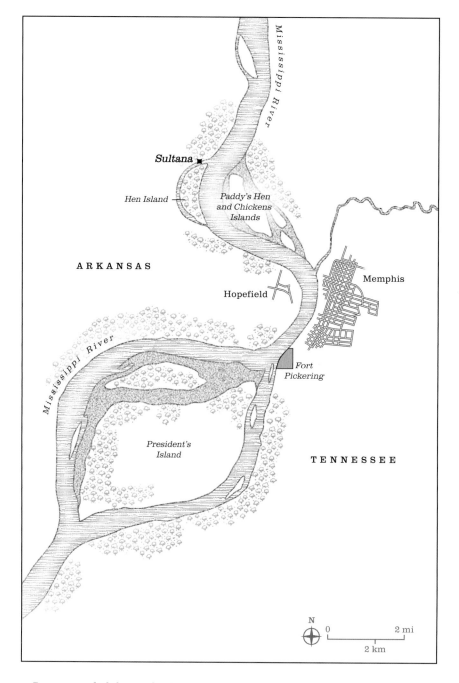

Rescuers combed the riverbanks north and south of Memphis searching for survivors.

and daughter." He saw DeWitt's grief-stricken face and heard him cry "at the sight of his dead mother and sister [Susan]." DeWitt's father, two brothers, two sisters, and his cousin were still missing. Desperate to find them, DeWitt wiped away his tears and joined the Foglemans in the rescue effort. He saved "no less than thirty lives." At that time, Hamilton had no idea of the whereabouts of his own brothers, John and Henry.

Other Arkansas residents joined the rescue. About a half mile downriver, at Mound City, James Berry woke his ten-year-old son, Louis, when he shouted, "A steamboat is afire up the river and a thousand people are drowning!" Berry ran toward the river to help. Between four and five o'clock in the morning, Louis and his mother dressed and hurried to the riverbank. To Louis, it seemed as bright as noontime. "The flames were leaping and plunging and breaking like the waves of the ocean. . . . I could hear the screams, prayers, and cries of a thousand men all at once, more than a hundred of whom were drowned in plain view of my mother and me," Louis recalled.

As the sun rose higher, the Berrys and their neighbors rescued a man "with both legs broken below the knee," possibly Daniel McLeod. They reported that they also found a little girl, about seven years old, "struggling in the water. She had on a life preserver, but it was on so low that her head was thrown downward." The neighbors tried to seize her, their actions nearly capsizing their boat. Unfortunately, they missed the girl, "who sank at once and was seen no more."

Louis's mother brought a big pot of coffee outside, and Louis and his cousin built fires to warm and dry the survivors. One of the men whom the Berrys rescued declared that he'd never been so cold in his life; he said he was shaking so hard, he feared he would shake the Berrys' house down.

Franklin Barton, one of the Berrys' neighbors, had recently been discharged from the Twenty-Third Arkansas Cavalry, a Confederate regiment. Ironically, less than a week before the *Sultana* departed from Memphis, Union troops had searched the area for Confederate soldiers engaged in guerrilla attacks on Union riverboats. During the search, the troops had destroyed all boats owned by people who lived in the area. As a result, very few boats were available for rescuing victims. But Barton had hidden his canoe before the Union soldiers arrived. He now launched it and paddled toward those who needed rescue. Barton later said "he did not care if they were Federal soldiers, humanity demanded that they should have help, and that he would do all in his power to help them."

Out on the river, Walter Elliott and his companion perched in a tree, chilled to the bone. They had pulled a young woman and two men out of the water, but none had survived. Elliott watched a man about forty yards away cling to a pole. Again and again, the man climbed up the pole, only to slide back into the water. Each time, he made less progress than the time before. He was finally exhausted to the point where he could do no more than tip his head back to keep his chin above water. Elliott felt certain the man would die. And then he saw something that he had never thought would make him happy: a Confederate uniform. It was Franklin Barton. (At that time, most people owned very few changes of clothes. Any warm garment, such as a jacket, was used until it wore out. Barton's Confederate jacket may have been his only heavy garment and would have protected him that chilly, wet morning.) Elliott yelled to Barton and pointed to the man grasping the pole. Barton rescued the man and then returned for Walter Elliott and his companion.

Barton, Berry, and their neighbors also rescued Ben Davis, Albert King, and Ann Annis. They wrapped them in quilts and warmed them near a fire. King was relieved to see George Hill, one of his comrades from the 100th Ohio, enter the house a short while later. He joined King and Ann. As the three talked, Ann "drew a ring from her finger [and] handed it to me [King] saying that all the valuables she had with her on the *Sultana* were lost excepting that ring, and it was all she could at the time offer me as a token of reward."

On the Tennessee shore of the river, local people were equally busy rescuing survivors. R. K. Hill and William Boardman, who worked just north of Memphis, had a small boat. They paddled to the scene and brought man after man to shore as quickly as they could. When they found the bodies of men who had perished, they laid them across logs in the driftwood so their bodies might be collected, possibly identified, and buried.

Surrounded by dense early-morning fog, people shivered in the cold water and in the flooded brush. They feared that rescue boats might never find them.

BIG BOATS JOIN THE RESCUE

William Alwood, chief mate on the steamer *Bostona II,* first saw the orange glow when his boat was about a mile upriver. Until the *Sultana* came into view, he thought Memphis was burning. Alwood arrived just as the smokestacks fell. Everywhere in sight, people struggled in the river. Immediately, the *Bostona II*'s crew lowered their yawl. Captain Watson directed his men to throw overboard anything that might assist the drowning people — gangplanks, tables, chairs, firewood, even bales of hay.

"Our yawl made nine trips while we were floating down stream bringing in at each trip from four to five persons," Alwood said. An exhausted Stephen Gaston, his arms and legs cramped with cold, was among them.

Some of the *Sultana*'s crew fled the wreck in a lifeboat with no regard for passengers' lives. William Rowberry, the *Sultana*'s first mate, behaved differently. After the *Bostona II*'s crew rescued him, they urged him to seek hot coffee and warmth in the boat's cabin. Rowberry refused. Instead, he remained in the yawl and rescued more men, including a soldier from Ohio. The man later praised Rowberry, saying he "did not cease his efforts in caring for others as long as there were any found needing assistance."

"We also used our lines in bringing persons to the boat," Alwood recalled. Unfortunately, one of these efforts failed. They lowered a rope to a young man — a soldier, they assumed — whose arms, while wrapped around a plank, also cradled two little girls, perhaps seven and nine years old. As he reached for the line, the girls slipped from his grasp. Abandoning his own rescue, the young man repeatedly dived after the girls. But the current swept them away. Exhausted, the soldier barely kept his head above water. Just as he went under, a small boat pulled him from the water. The *Bostona II*'s crew saved 200 to 250 people.

But Captain Watson realized that hundreds of victims still remained in the water. There was no way the *Bostona II* could rescue all of them. Making a difficult decision, Watson ordered his men to halt rescue operations. Ordering the engines at full steam, he raced his boat downriver (passing by such men as Robert Hamilton and Nicholas Karns) and sounded the alert that more help was needed.

As news of the disaster spread, every available steamboat joined the search for victims. Among them were steamboats that had been purchased or commandeered by the government and refitted as gunboats for the war. Taking to the river, gunboats gathered victims who struggled in the water or were stranded on drifts of wood and in trees. Their small boats collected survivors from local rescuers along both shores.

According to officer of the deck William Michael, the gunboat USS *Tyler* was at the navy yard in Memphis, six miles south of the disaster. Those on board, including Frances Ackley, were drawn to the scene when they heard victims crying for help. Frances, against her husband's wishes, joined the rescue efforts. While Frances and others set out in one of the *Tyler*'s cutters, or rowboats, William Michael took charge of another. He recalled one young man who "clutched the limb of a tree so tightly that we could not force him to let go his hold. We took the limb and man aboard together." The *Tyler*'s crew continued their rescue efforts "till all was hushed upon the surface of the river."

The gunboat USS Tyler *was a converted steamboat. Frances Ackley, whose husband was an officer on the* Tyler, *boarded one of its cutters to rescue* Sultana *survivors.*

At about 4 a.m., approximately seven miles downriver from the disaster scene, Thomas Love was on watch on the deck of the gunboat USS *Essex*. "I heard the cries of drowning men calling for help," said Love. He roused acting ensign James Berry (not related to the Berry family at Mound City) from sleep. Horrified by the agonizing cries of people in the river, Berry took immediate action. "I ordered all the boats manned . . . and we went out to the middle of the river," he later stated. But finding victims in the overcast, predawn hours was hard. It was impossible to see even twenty feet ahead. "The shrieks of the wounded and drowning men were the only guide we had."

As Berry rowed toward shore with victims, the crack of gun-shots sounded and bullets splashed into the water. Fort Pickering, a federal fort perched on the river bluff in the southernmost section of Memphis, was on high alert against river attacks by Confederate guerrillas. The sentries had orders to shoot at all small boats. Unaware of the disaster, the sentry had fired at Berry's rescue boat and then ordered him ashore.

The ensuing argument and explanation of the crisis wasted valuable rescue time. Berry resumed his rescue efforts, only to find himself under fire again. "Before we had taken in half of the men

The crew of the Essex, *another of the gunboats that aided the rescue, spent many hours searching for survivors.*

[surrounding us] another shot was fired from the fort, and came whistling over our heads." This time, Berry and his men disregarded the threat to their lives and continued their rescue mission. During the following hours, they removed sixty men and one woman from the river.

Meanwhile, Thomas Love and his men, in another of the *Essex*'s small boats, continued their search for survivors. "All that day we found men almost dead, hanging to the trees about two miles out into the river, and among those that I rescued was one man so badly scalded that when I took hold of his arms to help him into the boat, the skin and flesh came off his arms like a cooked beet," said Love. "I lost my hold on him but soon caught him again, and with help he was got into the boat and saved from a watery grave."

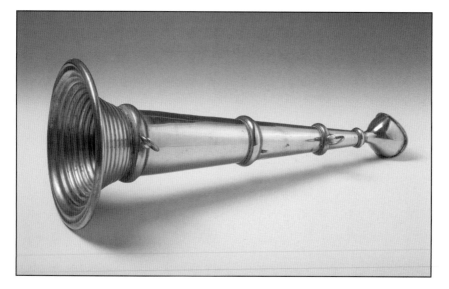

This speaking trumpet amplified the voice of the executive officer serving on the Essex *so all of the crew could clearly hear his orders.*

The men in both of the *Essex's* small boats worked all morning. When they no longer saw people in the river, they rowed into swampy areas and searched for victims who had reached land and needed help. Three miles south of Memphis, they delivered William Lugenbeal—still floating in his alligator box—onto the *Essex's* deck. Lugenbeal asked his rescuers to haul the box on board, too.

Commercial packet boats also responded to the call for aid. In many cases, these steamers picked up men and women who had been rescued by others and carried them to Memphis.

By noon on April 27, the *Memphis Argus* reported, 110 enlisted men, ten officers, four women, and fifteen citizens had been rescued, and more were on the way to shore. Although the sentries at Fort Pickering had, amid confusion, fired on the gunboat *Essex's* yawl, the situation quickly changed. Nearly one hundred survivors were taken to the fort. There, soldiers of the Third United States Colored Artillery built fires, erected temporary shelters, and provided hot coffee. Twenty-five of the severely injured victims were conveyed to the Third Artillery's hospital at the upper end of the fort, where the company surgeon attended to them.

As the day wore on, boats of all sizes delivered a steady stream of survivors, many of them badly burned, to Memphis. According to military records, eight hundred survivors were taken to Memphis's wharf. Two-thirds of the people on board the *Sultana* were still missing or dead; the captain, Cass Mason, was among them. While rescue efforts continued, ambulances and wagons carried the exhausted, chilled, and burned survivors to places where they received nursing and medical care.

CHAPTER 9

A GRIM SEARCH

BECAUSE TRAINS and boats could easily reach Memphis, it was a logical place to establish hospitals for ill and injured soldiers. After the Union captured control of Memphis from the Confederates in 1862, it became a medical center for Union soldiers. During the war, the citizens of Memphis often responded to pleas for "linen and cotton for bandages," so they were ready when survivors from the *Sultana* started arriving in town. Women brought warm drinks, blankets, and clothes from homes and nearby stores. Representatives from the Sanitary Commission brought more clothes, which the survivors — most of whom wore little or no clothing — gratefully accepted. Some of the citizens offered housing for the survivors who did not require hospitalization.

As Nicholas Karns walked through the crowd of men and women standing on the Memphis wharf, he covered his face with his hands and "wept like a school boy." He later said that he didn't know if his tears were from shame at his lack of clothes and physical condition or from joy. An ambulance carried him to a hospital.

HOSPITAL CARE

More than 520 survivors were transported to Memphis's six hospitals, brick buildings that had operated as hotels or business establishments before the war. Four hospitals — Gayoso, Overton, Adams, and Washington — received most of them. On May 2, the *Cincinnati Daily Commercial* reported that one man's body recovered by a steamer's yawl "was so horribly scalded that not the size of half a dollar of skin was left on the whole body." Tragically, this was true for many of the men who were closest to the *Sultana*'s boilers when they exploded. About three hundred survivors died from their burns while hospitalized. Sam Clemens, the *Sultana*'s second engineer, who had been on duty when the boilers burst, was severely scalded. Doctors cared for him as best they could, but he died less than a day later.

In 1861, the recently completed Overton Hotel became a military hospital for Confederate soldiers. After federal forces captured Memphis, injured and sick Union and Confederate soldiers were treated there. About ninety people rescued from the Sultana *received care at Overton Hospital.*

Burned and exhausted, Ann Annis lay helpless in Overton Hospital. She prayed that her husband, Harvey, and daughter Isabella were among the survivors. Ann pleaded with the nurses for news. At last, a nurse told her that she had overheard a soldier speaking about the disaster. The soldier remembered seeing a man and a little girl who were floating downstream, holding on to a window. He thought the child was wearing pink clothing. Ann knew Isabella had been wearing a pink nightgown. Further questioning the nurse, Ann learned the man and child had been heading toward an eddy. The child slipped off the window and sank in the swirling water. When she did, the man dived after her, and the soldier saw neither of them again. Ann believed that the window was part of the door Harvey had removed from its hinge to use as a raft and was convinced the soldier had seen her family. Widowed for the third time, Ann remained in the hospital for nearly two weeks. The women of Memphis came to her aid, supplying her with clothes and extra care. Ann returned to Wisconsin and her other children on May 11.

After he was rescued by the *Bostona II* and brought to Memphis, an ambulance transported Stephen Gaston to Overton Hospital. His arms and legs, cramped from the cold river, were scraped raw from his struggles to escape from beneath debris on the *Sultana*. He remained in the hospital for three days. (Gaston's friend William, who had disappeared after the explosion, survived and was treated at Washington Hospital.)

Nicholas Karns slowly regained strength under the care of Overton's physicians and nurses. Women of the Christian Aid

Society supplied him with "an old pair of pants, which had formerly belonged to an artilleryman," but when he was released from the hospital, he still had no shoes. He sat under a shade tree and tried to plan a way to travel home without boarding a boat.

A surgeon at Adams Hospital examined Daniel McLeod's fractured legs. He determined that he could set the two broken bones in McLeod's left leg. Unfortunately, the bones in his right leg — the one badly damaged at the Battle of Shiloh — were in worse condition. The surgeon told him that "it was no use trying to save [his] right leg . . . and that he would have to cut it off above the old wound." McLeod's fractured left leg healed after several weeks.

Doctors at Adams Hospital also tended Robert Hamilton, who was admitted chilled and with a bleeding head. His injuries were minor, and he was soon released. The next day, he began searching for his brothers John and Henry. Newspaper offices, army stations, and hospitals compiled lists of survivors. They also compiled lists of the dead when identification could be determined. Within hours, Robert and John, who also received only minor injuries, were reunited. Henry, along with at least 213 men from the Third Tennessee Cavalry, was dead.

Having jumped overboard without getting dressed, Simeon Chelf was chilled and itchy from the countless mosquito bites he had received while he awaited rescue. When he arrived at the Memphis wharf, he gratefully donned the clothes that were provided for him — a Confederate hat, a calico shirt, and a pair of red flannel drawers (long underwear). He was then taken by ambulance to the hospital at the Soldiers' Home. Seemingly fastidious, Chelf spread newspapers beneath him when he lay down "so as to keep [my] clothes clean." His injuries required hospitalization for eight to ten days.

Even as carriages and ambulances carried victims to the hospital, telegraph wires across the country buzzed with news of the disaster. Within forty-eight hours, the Memphis newspapers printed the first lists of the names of survivors and the hospitals where they had been admitted. In the next weeks, longer stories about the explosion—and even longer lists of people still missing or dead—appeared in newspapers in Ohio, Michigan, Indiana, Kentucky, and other Tennessee cities. These lists were, in many cases, the first information received by families that a loved one might be lost.

Walter Elliott had minor scalds on his face, and his lungs and throat were slightly scorched from inhaling heat and smoke. He was admitted to a hospital, most likely an officers' hospital, where he was treated and released. Elliott later returned to the wharf, where row upon row of coffins lined the cobblestones. There Elliott met George Safford, a survivor from the Tenth Indiana Cavalry. Safford's father, an agent with the Indiana Sanitary Commission, had traveled to Vicksburg to care for his son as he journeyed home on the *Sultana*. After the explosion, the Saffords floated in the river, clinging to a stateroom door. A horse separated them when it leaped from the burning boat and crashed on top of their makeshift raft. Since then, George had been unable to locate his father. Elliott and George Safford opened more than one hundred coffins to search for Mr. Safford's remains. When they didn't find Mr. Safford's

DAILY COMMERCIAL.

SATURDAY, APRIL 29.

LATEST BY TELEGRAPH

Our Special Dispatches.

APPALLING DISASTER.

EXPLOSION OF THE SULTANA

Eight Miles Above Memphis.

OVER 2,200 SOULS ON BOARD.

1,500 LIVES LOST.

MOSTLY PAROLED PRISONERS.

Statement by the Survivors.

Suspicion that the Explosion was Caused by a Torpedo in the Shape of a Lump of Coal.

Headlines in the Cincinnati Daily Commercial *informed citizens of the latest news about the disaster. Hundreds of Ohio families desperately awaited word about their loved ones.*

body, the two men went to a newspaper office, seeking news of Mr. Safford's whereabouts. "We visited the office of a morning paper, where I for the first time [since my capture at Nashville] gave my real name and command," Elliott recalled. There, George Safford received good news: his father had been found, unconscious, on the shore of an island twelve miles south of Memphis. Although injured, he was alive. George Safford caught the first boat south and was reunited with his father.

On May 3, Michael Dougherty wrote in his new diary, begun on April 12, the day that he left Andersonville Prison, "I am one of the lucky ones who escaped the sad disaster. I was well taken care of when I arrived [in a Memphis hospital] about a week ago." Soon after, he began his cross-country journey home to Philadelphia, Pennsylvania, where he, "more dead than alive . . . crippled with rheumatism and scurvy," was with "great joy" reunited with his mother and sister.

Back along the Mississippi, pieces of the *Sultana* littered the riverbank, some washing ashore miles downriver. As the flood-water abated, more objects came into view. In the woods among rubble from the wreck, officers of the steamer *Rose Hambleton* found Elethia Spikes's family Bible. It noted that the family lived in Assumption Parish, Louisiana. It recorded the date she and Samuel had married, October 31, 1837, and listed the names of twelve members of the family.

HEARTBREAK

The day after the explosion, reporters visited the wreck site. The *Sultana*'s blackened hull lay submerged in about twenty feet of water. About thirty bodies floated up out of the wreckage. In the days after the tragedy, the grim harvest of bodies continued. Charred remains of victims, some pulled from the water by John Fogleman and neighbors, lay onshore, waiting to be transported to Memphis. The steamer *Jenny Lind* collected dozens of bodies and brought them to the Memphis wharf.

A weakened Seth Hardin did not require hospital care. Instead, dressed in borrowed clothes, he sought accommodations in a hotel in downtown Memphis. The clerk refused to let Hardin have a room on the grounds that he had no money, no baggage, and looked bedraggled. Hardin found another hotel, whose employees had more compassion.

As the days passed, Seth Hardin searched all of the hospital wards. He visited one army office after another, asking if anyone had reported finding a young woman. He placed a "reward notice in the *Memphis Daily Bulletin* offering $100 [about $1,500 in modern currency] for the recovery of his wife's body." Hardin accompanied a group of men on a tugboat to the *Sultana*'s hull on May 10 to look for Hannah's body. Two days later, Hardin received word that a woman's body had been found along the river south of Memphis. He and several other men searching for lost family or friends hired the *Jenny Lind* and traveled downriver. Among them was the father of Henry Ingraham, one of the *Sultana*'s two pilots. Since the explosion, Mr. Ingraham had gone every day to the river and searched for his son. That day, the searchers found five bodies, including two whose clothes suggested that they had been deckhands on the *Sultana*. On board the *Jenny Lind,* people "could see tears rolling down Mr. Ingraham's face when he would pick up a body." None of the remains they found could be identified—the body reported to Hardin was not, in fact, a woman's body. All the searchers knew for certain was that none of the five bodies they found was Hannah Hardin or Henry Ingraham. After jotting down general descriptions—hair color, height, and, if present, clothing—the searchers buried the victims and marked the graves with wooden rails.

For days and weeks afterward, people found bodies in the river. Five days after the explosion, crewmen on board the USS *Tyler* saw bodies afloat in the river. Burying the remains where they found them was impossible due to the river's flooded banks. And the remains were too decomposed to bring on board. Regretfully, they left the bodies where they were.

Steamboat engineer Phineas Parks couldn't avoid the bodies. "The most horrible sight I saw during my whole service was immediately after that calamity. At the time I was Acting Engineer of the USS *Vindicator* . . . and while at anchor in the Mississippi River [she] would catch the driftwood [in her paddle wheels], which made it necessary to clear her wheels every day. When clearing the wheels after the *Sultana* disaster we would find them clogged with dead bodies from the *Sultana*."

Identifying the victims was an overwhelming task. Attempts to identify the dead led to rumors that people were robbing the bodies of their possessions. Yet checking pockets for papers or other possessions—a watch, diary, or family photo—was necessary, since these items might help identify a victim. If Arkansan John Fogleman had not opened the coat of one body he recovered, he never would have found the dead man's name — William Cruddis — written on a piece of paper and pinned inside. (Since identification tags were not issued during the Civil War, soldiers often tucked a piece of paper with their name on it inside their clothes so they could be identified if they were killed in battle.) The Memphis papers reported that rings that could not be removed were buried with the dead, an oversight that resulted in some victims being left anonymous who might otherwise have been identified.

Many of the remains brought to Memphis were burned beyond recognition. As days passed, the hope for identifiable remains decreased because of decomposition and scavenging animals. Unless a body had a distinctive feature, such as a tattoo, or unusual clothing, even a general description of the remains became difficult if not impossible.

Yet family members still hoped that a missing loved one would be found. Major William Fidler of the Sixth Kentucky Cavalry was one of the missing. His brother placed a reward notice in the *Memphis Argus* for any information about him. The notice included a detailed physical description of William and mentioned that he carried valuable papers and a gold pocket watch and wore a heavy gold ring. The family offered a substantial monetary reward for information and promised that the person who found his remains could keep the two gold items. Other families placed similar notices.

Rumors also circulated about Cass Mason, the *Sultana*'s captain. A $200 reward was offered for his body. On May 6, a story on the front page of New Orleans's *Times-Picayune* reported that he had survived and was recuperating in a house in Arkansas. An army representative and an agent from the Memphis and St. Louis Packet Company boarded the *Jenny Lind* "and made a diligent search, consuming the entire day . . . but unfortunately were unable to discover or hear anything of him." Mason's body was never recovered.

At least one person received hopeful news. On April 30, the *Memphis Argus* reported that DeWitt Spikes had received news that a boy who gave his last name as Spikes had been rescued by some Confederate soldiers on the Arkansas shore. DeWitt made plans to go up and investigate. Whether the report was true and the brothers were reunited is not known. The explosion orphaned DeWitt. He had been present when the bodies of his mother, Elethia, and his sister Susan were recovered. He saw to their burial in Elmwood Cemetery, one of Memphis's oldest burying grounds, where other victims were buried. But his father, two sisters, his cousin, and at least one, maybe two, brothers were still missing and presumed dead.

Burying the dead became an ongoing process as more remains were found. Dozens of badly decomposed bodies, including that of a baby, were buried without coffins on two of the islands near the *Sultana*'s charred hull. Hundreds more were interred in Elmwood Cemetery. Two years later, many of the soldiers' graves were opened to move their remains to the National Cemetery, a military burial ground also in Memphis. The name of each identified soldier was written in chalk on top of his coffin. A heavy rain fell during the course of the move and washed away the names. Almost all of the *Sultana*'s victims buried in the National Cemetery lie in graves marked "Unknown." John Clark Ely and William Cruddis are among the handful of the *Sultana*'s soldiers whose graves are marked by name.

KIND STRANGERS

Many disaster survivors said that help from kind strangers was a ray of hope that sustained them through a very dark time. The citizens of Memphis — Confederate and Union sympathizers alike — continued to put political differences aside as they tended to the victims.

The mayor of Memphis housed survivors in his home. A saloon-keeper provided several men with suits of clothes and also paid their hotel bills. The Chicago Opera Troupe, which had traveled from Vicksburg to Memphis on the *Sultana,* held a benefit performance and donated the proceeds to a relief fund established for the survivors. The New Memphis Theater did likewise. Parishioners from two churches contributed money to the fund. In a show of support for fellow soldiers, the men in a Union cavalry regiment stationed nearby took up a collection and added it to the relief fund. The fund gathered a total of $1,183.90 (about $17,700 in modern currency). While it was not enough to aid all the survivors, those in charge of distributing the funds identified twenty-three people "whose serious injuries and losses" singled them out as especially deserving assistance. DeWitt Spikes was given $200; Daniel McLeod was given $100. The *Memphis Bulletin* reported that the officers and men from the gunboat *Essex* gave $1,000 to a woman survivor "who was left alone in the world as husband, child, and sister were lost." According to the newspaper, her husband had been an officer on a gunboat.

While Memphis buried the dead, survivors resumed their journeys north. The thought of boarding another steamboat terrified them. Yet steamboats offered the fastest trip north to Ohio, where the men would begin the process of mustering out of the army.

Nicholas Karns had not included a boat ride in his plans for travel. The army decided otherwise. A few days after his release from the hospital, he was ordered to board the steamer *Belle Memphis.* "The thoughts of getting on another boat was a horror to me. If it had been reasonable that I could have made the trip . . . afoot I never would have embarked on another boat." But he had no choice. "I made my way to the bow of the boat, lay down in a coil of rope, and never got out of there until we reached Cairo the next day."

William McFarland, who traveled on the steamer *St. Patrick,* agreed. "I dreaded getting on a steamboat for fear of another explosion. Adopting what I suppose was the safest plan, I crawled into the yawl hanging over the stern of the boat . . . and never left my quarters until I arrived at the wharf at Evansville [Indiana]. . . . Every time the boat would escape steam or blow the whistle I prepared to jump, supposing an explosion was about to take place."

When the men reached shore, they completed their journeys via train or other wheeled vehicles, during which many of the paroled prisoners again experienced the kindness of strangers who wanted to help survivors of the explosion.

After one survivor transferred to a train in Illinois, he decided to stretch his legs while the train stopped early one morning in a small town. As the soldier walked past "a large, fine looking" house, a man came out and invited him in. Inside, nine more *Sultana* survivors had gathered in the sitting room, "all waiting for breakfast." A further surprise followed. "After the meal was over the man of the house provided himself with 10 one-dollar bills and gave one to each of us," the dumbfounded, yet grateful, soldier recalled.

(In modern currency, this would be the equivalent of about $15, more than enough to buy another good meal on the men's journeys home.)

The train carrying Robert Hamilton and Nicholas Karns to Ohio made a stop in Mattoon, Illinois. At that point, the men had not eaten for twenty-four hours. Hamilton commented, "On arriving at Mattoon we were met by the citizens of the surrounding country with wagon loads of provisions, the best that the country afforded. The vast multitude manifested their sympathy for us through speeches made by chosen orators. Never shall I forget seeing the tears shed by the stoutest hearts on that occasion."

Most of the survivors continued by train to Camp Chase in Ohio, where they would be officially mustered out of the army. Some, like bugler Stephen Gaston, reunited with family along the way. When his train stopped in his hometown, Terre Haute, Indiana, he managed a quick trip to his house before the train continued north. Walter Elliott, also from Indiana, wanting to ensure that the men received a welcome as equally warm as the one they received in Mattoon, sent telegrams to the governor of Indiana and the mayor of Terre Haute. A "dinner worthy of my grand old native state" was waiting when the men arrived, Elliott declared.

After Nicholas Karns was discharged from Camp Chase on May 11, he made a beeline home to McArthur, Ohio. His father picked him up at the train station. When his mother ran out from the house to welcome him home, he didn't know which of them had more tears rolling down their cheeks. And he thought, "No more screeching of shells or . . . crackling flames of a burning ship to haunt me in my dreams. I was safe at home."

Michael Dougherty, Robert Hamilton, Stephen Gaston, and Walter Elliott all returned home. John Ely and many more did not. In a report dated May 19, 1865, the commissary general of prisoners, Brigadier General William Hoffman, concluded that the total lost on the *Sultana* was 1,238. He based his figure on the number of people rescued and did not include the nearly three hundred survivors who later passed away in the hospitals. In a record book among the files of the Memphis Customs office, alongside the *Sultana*'s entry, a later notation added the phrase "Burned [on the Mississippi] and 1,600 persons perished," a number that the Customs Service later revised to 1,537. Confusion reigned as men who were reported as living proved to be dead and vice versa. Historians still comb old records, trying to reach a more accurate count for the number of dead.

For the survivors and the families of the dead, the number of people who died was not the most important question. The question they wanted answered was *Why?*

CHAPTER 10

WHY?

IN THE WAKE of the horrendous disaster, a number of people tried to determine what caused it. Within twenty-four hours, men on a tugboat visited the wreck site. When they sorted through the submerged debris, an agent from a steamboat company found what looked to him like a piece of an artillery shell that had been subjected to great heat. Had someone intent on sabotage put it in among the *Sultana*'s coal, where it lay until an unsuspecting crewman shoveled it into the furnace and it exploded?

A number of people believed a rebel plot was responsible. On May 3, 1865, the *Cleveland Daily Leader* reported that "a certain eternally-infamous villain named Joseph Stinson" had offered to destroy Union boats during the war if he and his agents were paid for it. The column's author wrote that these men had already burned one boat, the *J. H. Russell,* on the Mississippi River, and he believed that "the same diabolical spirit . . . is still at work, and that the scoundrels who destroyed the *J. H. Russell* also destroyed . . . the *Sultana.*"

As investigations continued, the *Sultana*'s first mate, William Rowberry, having heard rumors of sabotage, expressed the opinion that "a torpedo shaped like a lump of coal must have caused the explosion." Coal torpedoes did exist during the Civil War. Cleverly disguised to look like a lump of coal, these iron bombs, the size of a man's fist, contained several ounces of gunpowder.

When Seth Hardin visited the wreck, he was in the company of army personnel who were charged with investigating the explosion. He helped them retrieve a piece of iron from the front end of one of the *Sultana*'s boilers. The force of the explosion had torn the metal and bent it out of shape. The investigators said the severely burned piece proved "beyond a doubt, that the boilers were in a very bad

Even a small coal torpedo could set off an explosion. Gunpowder was poured inside the iron cast. A screw plug prevented the powder from spilling out, but it had two small holes in it to enable the explosion. Bits of melted wax, pitch, and coal dust, used to help disguise the torpedo, still cling to the exterior of the one on the left.

condition." They concluded that the piece of the boiler "dissipates the idea that a shell was the cause of the explosion."

Salvagers scoured the wreck for iron and machinery that might be reused or sold. Six months after the explosion, wreckers found and removed one of the inner boilers. It was the only one salvageable; the other three had been completely blown to bits by the explosion's tremendous burst of steam energy.

In 1888, coal-torpedo rumors resurfaced after St. Louis resident William Streeter said he spoke with a man who was a "notorious Confederate . . . blockade-runner." The man had escaped from St. Louis's military prison and journeyed south to wait for the war's end. He claimed that he had smuggled a coal torpedo on board the *Sultana* while it was at the Memphis wharf and said that he put the torpedo "in front of the boilers for the express purpose of the destruction of the boat." A number of *Sultana* survivors believed Streeter's story.

Henry Richards, who was an assistant engineer on the *Sultana*, was on leave at the time of the explosion. In response to Streeter's story, Richards refuted the torpedo rumor. Knowing that similar rumors had circulated prior to his leave, Richards said, "The greatest care was exercised in firing [up the *Sultana*'s furnace], and the coal was broken to small bits for the reason that a tip had been furnished that there would be an effort to blow up the vessel. The negroes who shoveled the coal were especially careful, as they were filled with the dread that some fiendish effort would be made." Richards believed the failure lay in the boilers' construction.

Whether it was due to sabotage or boiler failure, such a

catastrophic loss of life, particularly one that killed so many soldiers, demanded that the army investigate.

ARMY INVESTIGATIONS

Anticipating an investigation of the disaster, General Cadwallader Washburn traveled to Memphis and, only a few hours after the first people were rescued, appointed three officers to act as a court of inquiry. Washburn's court began taking testimony before lunchtime on April 27. Three of the *Sultana*'s officers — pilot George Kayton, first mate William Rowberry, and second engineer Samuel Clemens — were among the first to testify. Clemens's testimony was recorded as he lay dying in a hospital bed. In his statement, Clemens said he "considered the boilers safe after the repairs at Vicksburg. Though the work was apparently well done, think it very probable the explosion was caused by defective repairs. The boat rolled considerably owing to her being very light." Upon reflection, he may have realized that the repairs were insufficient or defective. Clemens died shortly afterward.

The Washburn Commission interviewed survivors who provided eyewitness testimony of what the conditions were like on board the *Sultana* after they left Vicksburg and what happened during the disaster. It also collected testimony from people who aided in the rescue effort. The information gathered offered a partial picture of the disaster. But Washburn's officers needed to know more about how and why so many men had been placed on the *Sultana* and who had authorized it; they wanted to further investigate the repair work done on the boiler. The court adjourned its investigation in Memphis and went to Vicksburg, where they questioned a variety of people, including the boiler repairman, men from other steamboats, Colonel Reuben Hatch, and captains George Williams, Frederic Speed, and William Kerns.

Even as the Washburn court of inquiry started questioning people in Vicksburg, General Dana, who was stationed in town, began his own investigatory commission. He appointed General Smith to head it. (Smith was one of the officers whom Kerns had asked more than once to transfer prisoners from the *Sultana* onto the empty *Pauline Carroll*.) Dana's commission interviewed only five witnesses. Miles Sells, the steamboat agent who met with Captain Mason and George Williams to discuss prisoners being obtained for the *Sultana,* was one of the five. William Kerns was another, but he did not testify in person as the other four men had. Instead, his testimony was received in writing and was limited to a handful of questions.

One of the men who testified before the Dana Commission was another agent from a steamboat company. He swore that Lieutenant Tillinghast (from the Quartermaster's Department) had told him that the *Sultana*'s captain, Mason, would have given him (Tillinghast) money if Mason had known Tillinghast would take it. But that Mason said, "Not having [Tillinghast's] measure, he had made it all right anyhow." This alleged statement suggests that Mason bribed someone to get passengers. But who? Dana submitted the five testimonies collected by his commission to the officers conducting the Washburn Commission.

While the Washburn and Dana Commissions gathered

information in Vicksburg, the secretary of war, Edwin Stanton, in Washington, D.C., ordered Brigadier General William Hoffman to go to Memphis, investigate, and issue a report directly to him. By the time Hoffman reached Memphis, during the first week of May, most of the survivors had been released from hospitals and were on their way north. Hoffman interviewed some of the remaining people, Ann Annis among them, and then continued to Vicksburg. When General Hoffman arrived, the Washburn and Dana Commissions turned the testimonies from their courts of inquiry over to him.

After reading the steamboat agent's testimony about bribery (from the Dana Commission), as well as mentions of suspected bribery in testimonies given by Speed and Williams (to the Washburn Commission), the Hoffman Commission probed the issue further. Lieutenant Tillinghast was called to testify. In his testimony, he made a number of statements about bribery. He implicated men in the Quartermaster's Department (inadvertently including himself), steamboat agents, and Frederic Speed.

Hoffman received more testimony from a number of individuals about the loading of the boat and the conditions on board. For clarification, he recalled Speed, Kerns, and Williams to answer additional questions. Despite Speed's statement that as far as he knew, Reuben Hatch had chosen the *Sultana* as the boat to transport the prisoners, Hatch was not asked to return for further questioning.

After wrapping up his investigation in Vicksburg, Hoffman returned by train to Washington. Along his journey, he stopped and interviewed more survivors, including Nathan Wintringer (the *Sultana*'s chief engineer) in Pennsylvania.

Reading the many pages of testimony, Hoffman received a clear picture of the overcrowding. He read about the boiler's repair. He found contradictions in whether the repair was adequate or not. The boiler repairman testified that the patch used to repair the leaking boiler was not of the same thickness as the surrounding iron — it was thinner, and hence more likely to give way under high pressure. Wintringer, who had hired the repairman, said the boiler was fine.

Hoffman reread testimony about the water level inside the boilers. Men familiar with steamboats said that if the water level in a boiler was too low, the boiler would overheat and explode. Others said that if the boat had careened due to the overcrowding, the tilting would have affected the water level inside the boilers and led to an explosion. The *Sultana*'s pilot George Kayton and Ann Annis said the boat ran steady. Others said it careened. Hoffman wondered, If the water levels had been too low and the boat careened, might that have led to the tipping point that caused the explosion? No one seemed to know the answer.

Ultimately Hoffman decided that he could not issue a definitive statement as to what caused the explosion.

PROPER PUNISHMENT

When the secretary of war ordered Hoffman's court of inquiry, he directed Hoffman to "have all parties guilty of neglect or improper conduct in the matter arrested and report, that speedy trial and proper punishment may be had." Besides trying to determine the cause of the explosion, Hoffman needed to find out who bore the blame for loading so many soldiers onto the boat and why it had happened.

General Dana's and General Smith's ranks gave them ultimate control. An order from either one of them to divide the prisoners and put some on another boat would have superseded any order given by Hatch, Williams, or Speed. Yet they did nothing.

Colonel Reuben Hatch outranked captains Williams and Speed. The Quartermaster's Department, under Hatch's command, was responsible for selecting the specific means of transportation. Despite having met with the *Sultana*'s captain, plus steamboat agent Miles Sells and Williams and Speed, Hatch insisted that he had nothing to do with which boat was selected or the men who were loaded onto it. Hatch could have ordered men transferred off the *Sultana.* Yet he did nothing.

People speculated about why such a large number of men had been put on the *Sultana.* The *Chicago Tribune* — summing up the opinion of many — baldly stated: "The infernal machine that exploded the boiler and sent so many souls into eternity, carrying bereavement and mourning into thousands of our western homes, was undoubtedly the bribe — the greenbacks paid by the officers of the *Sultana* to the quartermaster for the transportation of the troops." People demanded that the guilty be held accountable. Louisiana's *Shreveport Weekly News* declared, "It cannot be pleaded . . . that there was no suspicion of danger, as the overburdened boiler itself sounded the note of warning before reaching Vicksburg. . . . This cannot be regarded as one of those accidents that could not have been avoided by proper precaution, and we hope it will be looked into and the guilty party found and punished without the least regard to his wealth or position."

WHAT CAUSES A BOILER TO EXPLODE?

In the 1800s, the science behind boiler explosions and what caused them was not clearly understood. Boilermakers believed that when a boiler was full of water, it could not explode. They thought that when the water level in a boiler got low, the iron sheets that formed the boiler overheated and got red-hot. Then, when water touched the red-hot sheet again, the water vaporized and created an overload of steam pressure that resulted in an explosion. Scientists now know that this is not the case.

So how and why did the *Sultana*'s boiler explode? Twenty-first-century boiler engineers have a theory, and water temperature provides only part of the answer. Three facts about water and energy provide key information needed to unlock the mystery.

The first fact is that there is a lot of energy stored inside a steam boiler. And almost all of that energy is stored in the water.

The second fact is that water boils at a different temperature when it is under pressure. The average air pressure at sea level on Earth is about 14.7 pounds per square inch. At sea level, water in an uncovered pan boils at 212° F (100° C).

But when pressure is added, it raises the boiling point of water. At the *Sultana*'s inspection on April 12, each of its four boilers was approved to operate at up to 145 pounds of pressure per square inch. Under that pressure, water boils at 363° F (184° C). Nathan Wintringer, the *Sultana*'s chief engineer, estimated that after the steamboat left Memphis, its boilers were operating under a pressure of 130 to 135 pounds. The temperature of the water inside its boilers was well over 300° F (149° C).

The third fact is that when water boils at a very high temperature (because it is under intense pressure) and the pressure drops — as would happen if a boiler starts to leak — the temperature of the water also drops. But for a short moment, the water remains hotter than the boiling point of water at the new, lower pressure. Because the water temperature is hotter than the boiling point at which water converts to steam at the lower pressure, it instantly converts to steam. When it does, it expands (1 cubic inch of water equals 1 cubic foot of steam). This suddenly repressurizes the boiler back to a higher level.

If a boiler has only a small leak, it can accommodate the gradual change in pressure that occurs, which gives the water time to cool. If, however, a large area of iron ruptures, a large amount of water instantly converts to steam as the pressure suddenly decreases. The tremendous force of the energy released will lead to a massive explosion that will rip a boiler and those alongside it to pieces. According to Wintringer, the *Sultana*'s iron patch measured 8 inches by 22 inches, so it was fairly large. And it was made from a sheet of iron that was thinner than the rest of the boiler. If the patch ruptured, a large leak would have resulted.

But the patch might not have been the root cause of the explosion. Engineers now know that the iron used to make steamboat boilers, believed to be good at the time, was actually of poor quality. The iron was very brittle, and became more so as it was repeatedly heated and cooled.

In addition, the Mississippi River itself contributed to the explosion. As a river flows, particles of sand and silt are suspended in the water, and the Mississippi is notoriously muddy. All steamboats filled their boilers with river water. As a result, the boilers got dirty. They had to be regularly cleaned inside to remove accumulated mud. In the case of the *Sultana,* each of whose boilers contained twenty-four tubular flues, it was impossible to remove all the mud. Within weeks, scale — an encrustation that formed from the dissolved minerals and naturally occurring chemicals contained in the river water — coated the bottom of the boilers and the exterior of the flues. The coating of scale acted as a layer of insulation between the boilers and their flues and the water they needed to heat. The fire burning beneath each boiler had to be stoked to provide more heat. When the boat was docked, the fires died and the iron boilers cooled. This established a pattern of heating and cooling that stressed and weakened the brittle iron. The *Sultana*'s deteriorated boilers were a ticking bomb counting down toward explosion.

What did the army investigators decide? After reviewing the testimony, Washburn's court came to these conclusions: First, repairs made to the boiler were insufficient but had not endangered the safety of the boat. Second, calm order had been maintained on board the boat, and the men were reasonably comfortable given the crowded conditions. And finally, although the number of men on board had not compromised the *Sultana*'s safety, there should have been fewer, especially since the *Pauline Carroll* was available. General Washburn censured the Quartermaster's Department for not carrying out its duties. He also censured Speed for assuming a duty — taking charge of transferring the men from Camp Fisk to the boat — that was not properly his but was, rather, the responsibility of George Williams.

Newspapers nationwide published Washburn's report. On May 24, the *Chicago Tribune*'s editors followed the printed report with their opinion: "This report reads very much like a studied attempt to conceal the guilty, and whitewash those who crowded 2,400 souls on a boat that ought not have received one-fourth of the number. The court [of inquiry] evidently resolved to deal gently with the murderers, and not hurt their feelings."

Hoffman's report to the secretary of war was more specific with regard to responsibility. It concluded that Hatch, Speed, Williams, and Kerns were all responsible, but that Hatch and Speed deserved the most blame. Hoffman believed they had not fulfilled their duty to see that the men had been properly treated. He also criticized General Smith for not personally visiting the wharf, noting that men would have been saved if Smith had carried out his duty.

The court-martial of Frederic Speed, the only person brought to trial for the Sultana *disaster, was held in Vicksburg's courthouse, built in 1858.*

In response to Hoffman's report — which included the testimonies from the Washburn and Dana Commissions — General Meigs, the quartermaster general of the U.S. Army, ordered that Hatch, Speed, and Kerns be tried before a military tribunal.

But that didn't happen. After months of military finger-pointing, Frederic Speed became the army's scapegoat. He was the only person whom the army tried for the *Sultana* disaster. Speed's court-martial trial began January 9, 1866, more than eight months after the boat sank. He was charged with "neglect of duty to the prejudice of good order and military discipline." This charge specifically meant that Speed had not used the Quartermaster's Department to provide the necessary and safe transportation for the prisoners. Further, it

At the end of a six-month-long military trial, Frederic Speed was found guilty of neglect of duty. The verdict was later reversed, and Speed was honorably discharged from service.

specified that Speed had assumed the duties of the Quartermaster's Department in directing that all of the prisoners should be transported on one boat, the *Sultana*. Speed pleaded not guilty.

Of the officers who had selected and loaded the *Sultana,* only Speed, Williams, and Kerns testified at the court-martial trial.

Generals Dana and Smith had resigned from the army the previous summer.

Lieutenant Tillinghast, whose allegations had opened the door to the subject of bribery, wasn't available; he was in Chicago, serving a jail sentence for forgery.

Three times the court subpoenaed Colonel Hatch to appear and testify. He ignored all the subpoenas. The court requested his arrest but was powerless to enforce the request because Hatch had been discharged from the army the previous summer. He was a civilian and, as such, was outside the military's jurisdiction. The trial continued without Hatch.

Six months later, in early June, the court announced its verdict for the charge against Speed: guilty.

Speed was on track for a dishonorable discharge from the army. Following procedure, the secretary of war, Edwin Stanton, sent the court's finding to the top man at the Bureau of Military Justice: Brigadier General Joseph Holt, the judge advocate general of the U.S. Army.

Holt reviewed all of the evidence — hundreds of pages of testimony from the Washburn, Dana, and Hoffman Commissions and the court-martial investigations — and made a decision that shocked many. He ruled that nothing Speed had done in transporting the prisoners should have left him in a position deserving of punishment. Holt felt that Speed was wholly subordinate to other officers; that he *had* used the services of Hatch and Kerns and had *not* overloaded the boat without authority — Hatch knew about it. Further, Holt ruled, overcrowding the boat had not led to the destruction of the *Sultana*. That, he believed, was the result of inadequate repairs to the boiler. He recommended that Speed be exonerated. Secretary of War Stanton reversed the court's verdict to one of not guilty. Speed was honorably discharged from the army on September 1, 1866.

More than a year after the *Sultana*'s destruction and the loss of more than fifteen hundred lives, the army — operating under Stanton's April 1865 directive to properly punish all parties guilty of neglect or improper conduct — declared who would be held responsible and punished.

No one.

CHAPTER II

A SAD TRUTH

THE JOURNEY HOME for the survivors was only a first step on what became for many a difficult recovery. Some of the survivors suffered debilitating injuries, which hampered their ability to work. As time passed and the survivors aged, the long-term physical effects of the disaster became apparent. Damage caused to the tissues that line the throat and lungs, a result of inhaling hot steam and breathing smoke, led to an increased susceptibility to respiratory ailments. For others, scar tissue from severe burns increasingly restricted mobility. When added to the effects of diseases that the men suffered — such as tooth loss from scurvy — while imprisoned at Andersonville and Cahaba, physical discomfort became chronic. The psychological scars can only be imagined.

COMPENSATION

The enlisted soldiers who traveled on the *Sultana,* whether they lived or died, were entitled to a pension from the army, a sum paid by the government to help them or their dependents financially. Obtaining the pension wasn't easy. Because the lists of men who boarded the trains at Camp Fisk and went on to the *Sultana* had been created as George Williams suggested and not in the standard way, no one knew exactly who was on the boat.

After the disaster, men left for the north at different times. Those who checked in at Camp Chase were recorded in the army records as alive. But some men neglected to report to Camp Chase; they simply returned home or to their unit. In these cases, the army did not know whether the soldiers were alive or dead.

At the end of the war, in a move to reduce paperwork and cost, the army issued a blanket general order that mustered out all soldiers in certain categories, such as those who were patients in hospitals or prisoners of war. This blanket order made no attempt to verify whether a man was actually alive. Ironically, as a result, the prisoners of war who died on the *Sultana* appear in army records as alive.

Due to confusion arising from the poor record keeping, some men who had boarded the *Sultana* were incorrectly listed as dead. In 1892, Chester Berry, a survivor who lived in Michigan, collected the stories of more than 130 survivors and published them as a book. In the account of his own survival, Berry wrote, "About two or three months [after I was reported alive] my mother received official notice from Washington that her son was killed upon the 'Sultana.'" When Berry applied for a pension, he had to provide written testimony that he was alive and indeed Chester Berry, and that his skull had been badly fractured during the disaster.

As the years passed, *Sultana* survivors felt that the federal government had neglected them and that, due to circumstances created by the disaster, they deserved additional compensation. Several times, the U.S. Congress introduced bills to financially help both survivors who were too disabled to do manual labor and the widows and children of the soldiers killed during the explosion. None of the bills was enacted. What is more, the government did not even erect a memorial marker to commemorate the disaster.

NEVER FORGET

The survivors never forgot the tragedy they had experienced, and they reached out to one another. In 1885 a group of them founded the *Sultana* Survivors' Association. They held the first meeting in Ohio. Survivors who attended lived predominantly in Ohio, Indiana, and Michigan. During the meeting they sang, prayed, shared picnic meals, and reminisced about their time in prison camps and on the *Sultana*. Afterward, they decided to hold a reunion annually. As the years passed, the families of soldiers who had died in the explosion began to attend, as did men who had participated in rescue efforts. Thomas Love—the crewman from the gunboat USS *Essex* who had grasped the hand of a severely burned man—attended the 1890 reunion. While there, he had the pleasure of shaking the hand of the man he had rescued.

Survivors also reached out to one another between reunions. In 1890, Marcellus Reynolds, who lived in Ohio, wrote a letter to the *Elyria Democrat* describing his experience on the

Sultana. He ended his letter by inviting other *Sultana* survivors to respond. Reynolds's article was reprinted in several Ohio newspapers. Survivor William Madden—the man who commended the *Sultana*'s first mate, William Rowberry, for rescuing victims despite being exhausted himself—lived nearly two hundred miles from Elyria. He read Reynolds's article and responded: "There is a kindred feeling, however, that only exists between those who shared the affliction of that terrible time. And now, Comrade Reynolds, it is enough for me to know that you are one of us. And as our number is so small, let us keep alive an association that will bring us annually together, keeping in memory that incident that shall bind us together."

Challenged by distance, expense, and difficulty of travel, survivors in Kentucky and Tennessee established their own annual reunions. In 1912, this group, led by the efforts of John Simpson, a survivor who was seventeen years old at the time of the explosion, and other members of the Third Tennessee Cavalry collected funds and commissioned a monument to the Tennessee prisoners who were on the *Sultana*. It stands on a hilltop in Knoxville's Mount Olive Cemetery. The front of the marker is carved with an image of the *Sultana*. The names of Tennessee prisoners who were on board the boat are inscribed on the monument. Private Charles Eldridge of the Third Tennessee Cavalry was the last known survivor of the *Sultana* disaster. He died on September 8, 1941, at age ninety-six.

One of the survivors' concerns was that the *Sultana* would be forgotten. In 1987, a new group, the Association of *Sultana*

Sultana survivor John Simpson of the Third Tennessee Cavalry headed the drive to erect this memorial to those who died in the Sultana *disaster. The monument, located in Knoxville, Tennessee, is inscribed on all four sides with the names of the dead and was dedicated in 1916.*

Descendants and Friends, formed, and it has held annual reunions every year since then. Descendants and other interested parties gather to remember the disaster, share stories, and educate people about what happened.

IN A LARGER SENSE

When the *Sultana* exploded, more lives were lost than when the *Titanic* hit an iceberg and sank forty-seven years later. Many people know about the *Titanic*. Why has the *Sultana*'s story — the worst maritime disaster in American history — largely faded into the past?

In many ways, the answer lies in the turmoil that existed in the United States in 1865. By April 27, 1865, Americans had suffered through four years of the Civil War. More than 750,000 men had died as a direct result of the war. Newspaper reports of battlefield deaths and casualties were printed regularly. In a terrible way, the nation had become numbed by death. And while the *Sultana* disaster was widely reported, war news from other areas of the country filled many more columns of newsprint.

Moreover, when the *Sultana* sank, the nation was still reeling from Abraham Lincoln's assassination. As the train carrying his body chugged from Washington, D.C., to Illinois, articles about his funeral cortège edged news about the *Sultana* to the second and third pages of most newspapers. And on April 26, the day before the *Sultana* exploded, Lincoln's assassin, John Wilkes Booth, was shot and killed. That event garnered headline news.

Immediately after the initial news of the explosion, newspaper articles reported that men from every state in the Union had been on board the doomed boat. As more information filtered in, it became apparent that this was not true. The overwhelming majority of the people on board were from Ohio, Tennessee, Indiana, Michigan, and Kentucky. In the 1860s, given the lack of rapid transport and instant communication, many people who lived along the Atlantic seacoast considered these states the fringe of the western frontier. For eastern papers, breaking news about events that occurred on the East Coast eclipsed coverage of a disaster that occurred in the Midwest. Aside from short articles reporting on the beginning and conclusion of Speed's trial, the *Sultana* story faded out of the news.

America's rich tapestry of history contains countless stories. On a loom created by a country at war with itself, the *Sultana*'s tale weaves together heroes and heroines, soldiers and civilians, technological advances and mechanical failures. The horrors of war, the acts of negligence, and the selfless acts of bravery found in the *Sultana*'s story occur today in parallel events: a war-torn nation, an overcrowded ferry, individuals who place profit above safety, and people who kindly aid suffering victims of disaster. Even though the *Sultana* sank more than 150 years ago, its story still resonates in a way that time cannot erase. Because of this, the tale of the *Sultana*, once heard, is one that people will remember.

EPILOGUE

THE MISSISSIPPI RIVER still flows south from Minnesota, meandering the final few hundred miles as it nears the Gulf of Mexico. But the river began to change its course in 1876, "leaving Vicksburg high and dry." In the area where the *Sultana* sank, just north of Memphis, Tennessee, its channel has shifted approximately two miles to the east since April 27, 1865. The island where the *Sultana*'s burning hull touched shore is now a low hill in a field planted with crops. But sometimes, after days of heavy rains or when northern ice melts, the river's current runs wild. And then, water once again surrounds the trees and buildings as it did the day so many people died.

MICHAEL DOUGHERTY received the Congressional Medal of Honor in 1897 for "most distinguished gallantry in action at Jefferson, Virginia, October 12, 1863." Under enemy fire he led his men in a charge to defend territory that prevented the enemy from flanking the Union forces. Dougherty published his diary in 1908.

He ends his book with the hope that future readers will discover his and other prisoner-of-war accounts and, by doing so, be "better able to appreciate the many blessings you now enjoy."

J. WALTER ELLIOTT returned home to Indiana. A widower before the war began, Elliott was reunited with his young daughter, who was being raised by relatives. He married for the second time in 1866. His second wife died less than a year later. Elliott practiced law, as he had before the war. Eventually he moved to Alabama, where he married for a third time in 1870. He and his wife, Betty, had five children. When Elliott retired from the law, he became a farmer and fruit grower.

JOHN CLARK ELY is buried in Memphis National Cemetery. Julia and the children eventually moved east, to Connecticut, where they lived with John's parents. Ely's descendants treasure the small black diary that holds John's memories of the last ten months of his life. It is not water-stained; the writing is clear. His last entry is on April 26, the day the *Sultana* docked in Memphis. Within hours, he was dead. Had he mailed the diary to Julia just before departing Memphis? Was it still in his pocket when his body was recovered? Julia knew how the diary reached home, but she died in 1873. The answer has been lost to history.

STEPHEN GASTON returned home to Indiana after the war. There he received the news that his older brother William had been killed in the war just about the time Stephen was captured and sent to Cahaba. Stephen became a locomotive engineer working for a flour mill. He and his wife had seven children and eventually moved to Texas.

ROBERT HAMILTON returned to Tennessee after he left Camp Chase and continued farming. He married and moved to Oregon but eventually settled in Oklahoma. He and his wife had two children. In 1879, Hamilton supplied the government with written character testimony and eyewitness statements regarding his roan mare and her requisition by Sherman's troops. On June 14, 1880, the U.S. government paid him $120, the amount Robert estimated was her monetary worth.

THE REMAINS OF THE *SULTANA* are buried beneath layers of sediment deposited by the river. Residents of Mound City, Arkansas, say that nearly twenty years into the twentieth century the boat's jack staff was still visible, poking up through the soil. In recent years, historians and scientists have used scientific instruments to search the area where they believe the wreckage lies. They have found pieces of metal that may have belonged to the boat. The area may also contain undiscovered remains of victims who were trapped within the *Sultana*'s burning hull. Under Arkansas law, a special archaeological act is required to excavate a site that could contain human remains. For now, there are no plans to excavate the site.

AUTHOR'S NOTE

Always a Civil War buff, I was gripped by the *Sultana*'s story from the first moment I heard about it, and the more I came to know about the experiences of the people on board, the more captivated I became. Realizing the *Sultana* disaster had been completely preventable saddened me. The chicanery, bribery, and greed infuriated me. The strength and resilience of the prisoners amazed me. I had to tell the story.

Everyone interested in the *Sultana* must seek out Chester Berry's book *Loss of the Sultana and Reminiscences of Survivors*. In 1892, he collected the stories of many survivors. Without them, we would have lost most of the eyewitness accounts of the disaster. I owe huge thanks to Jerry Potter (*The Sultana Tragedy: America's Greatest Maritime Disaster*), who sent me a transcription of John Clark Ely's diary and introduced me by e-mail to Gene Eric Salecker (*Disaster on the Mississippi: The Sultana Explosion*). Their phenomenal books about the *Sultana* were touchstones during every step of my research; their lists of the people on board the boat reflect *years* of meticulous research. Gene helped me understand steamboat construction, particularly that of the *Sultana,* and the logistics of transferring men from Camp Fisk to Vicksburg. His knowledge of the disaster is incomparable.

For anyone researching a historical event, it is always exciting to speak with descendants of people who experienced the event. In the case of the *Sultana,* I've been fortunate to hear family stories from Kenneth R. Hamilton, a descendant of one of the Hamilton brothers, and from Frank Fogleman and Frank Barton, whose ancestors rescued and recovered many victims. Helen Chandler and Mike Annis confirmed Isabella Annis's name and her death date from records in the Annis family Bible. Joseph Thatcher provided information about his ancestor Thomas Courtenay and his work developing the coal torpedo. I thank all of them for sharing their families' roles in history.

I couldn't have written this book without the help of an army of librarians. M'Lissa Kesterman at the Archives in the Cincinnati Museum Center and Laura Cunningham and Marilyn Umfress at the Memphis Public Library hauled countless boxes and folders of materials to me without complaint. Rebecca Bledsoe in West Memphis scanned a hard-to-find newspaper article and e-mailed it to me, as did Laura Cunningham. What would we do without librarians?

The *Sultana* Disaster Museum, in Marion, Arkansas, is a work in progress. To date, there are only two known photographs of the *Sultana*. The fourteen-foot model of the *Sultana*, painstakingly restored by Gene Eric Salecker, is a centerpiece exhibit that clarifies the boat's layout and helped me understand where my storytellers were during their time on board. Thanks to Rosalind O'Neal for showing my husband and me around the museum and its exhibits.

Norman Shaw is at the Knoxville helm of the Association of *Sultana* Descendants and Friends. He helped me contact people and suggested great research sources in Knoxville, particularly the Calvin M. McClung Historical Collection at the Knox County Public Library. Most important, Norman told me where to find the *Sultana* memorial in Mount Olive Cemetery in Knoxville. It stands as a labor of love, designed and placed by survivors who wanted to make certain that future generations would not forget the sacrifices of those who came before us. As I read the names inscribed on the memorial, I recognized many of the men whom I had come to know through my research. And so there was a connection between us.

The New Orleans riverfront seen in photographs and drawings from the nineteenth century in no way resembles the bustling industry that I saw along the twenty-first-century riverfront. But in Memphis, if you take the time to look, you can still see the cobblestone wharf. The Mississippi River was at flood stage when I visited Memphis. I can easily understand how the victims of the *Sultana* got confused about the shoreline. In Cincinnati, steep hills along the Ohio River make it very clear why the steamboats were built on the riverbank. It would have been impossible to launch them otherwise.

While the majority of graves in the Memphis National Cemetery are not associated with the *Sultana* disaster, many hundreds of them are. After paying my respects at John Ely's grave, I counted the white gravestones in several nearby rows. Doing some multiplication allowed me to envision how large an area would have been necessary to encompass the hundreds of white gravestones needed to mark the graves of the *Sultana*'s unidentified victims. I was stunned. Thanks to Amanda Rhodes-Wharton at Memphis National Cemetery and Kelly Sowell at Elmwood Cemetery (where Elethia and Susan Spikes are buried) for answering my questions about the burials of *Sultana* victims.

I have a son, and felt sorrow for the many mothers whose boys went off to fight. Two-fifths of all soldiers who fought in the Civil War were twenty-one or younger at the time they enlisted. Knowing that my great-great-grandfather suffered poor health for the rest of his life as a result of his service during the Civil War, I wondered about the physical health of the *Sultana* survivors after they returned home. But I wondered even more about their mental health. They survived the appalling conditions of prison camps and then a horrendous disaster. At that time, no one recognized post-traumatic stress; men were expected to go home and resume life as before. For many, I doubt that happened.

I must also take this opportunity to thank the Mississippi River. For thirty years, I have lived within hailing distance of it. I've seen it low and high, ice-sluggish and flood-flowing. In some places, buildings and pavement completely shroud the riverbanks; in other places, nothing but trees (and snags) line the banks, and it looks much as it did in the nineteenth century. In those places, I've been lucky to see an eagle and a pelican — seriously! Pelicans follow the river up from the south. Though I've seen the Mississippi many times, it took writing about the *Sultana* to get me on the water. My husband and I spent a lovely afternoon traveling on a steamboat up and down the stretch of the river near Dubuque, Iowa. The boat was a small stern-wheeler. I stood near the paddle wheel, less than one-fourth the size of the *Sultana*'s paddle wheels, and listened. It was noisy. I can only imagine what the *Sultana*'s wheels — even covered — sounded like when it was running fast. I loved it when the captain sounded the steam whistle. It's a sound that fills the ears and reverberates in the chest. Absolutely thrilling.

History and research are all about making connections. Each time a person discovers the *Sultana*'s story — even though it may be many years after the disaster — a connection is established between that person and the people who were on the boat. Maybe the *Sultana* connection will motivate that person to help a victim who has suffered a recent disaster. Maybe it will give someone the courage to protest against an unethical situation, an unfair business practice, or an action that exhibits questionable safety. Recognizing and acting in these cases make the *Sultana* relevant for people today. Perhaps that is the best way we can honor the memory of those who died on the *Sultana*.

GLOSSARY

BOILER: The iron cylinder in a steam engine that contains water as well as the flues.

BOW: The front of a boat.

BUCKET: One of the flat paddles on a steamboat's paddle wheel.

BULLY: An exclamation often used in the nineteenth century that means "hooray" or "terrific."

CABIN DECK: The deck above the main deck. It is where the *Sultana*'s passenger staterooms and the cabins for ladies and for gentlemen were located.

COMMISSARY: A military building where food is dispensed to soldiers.

COURT-MARTIAL: A court trial held for people in the military who are accused of breaking military law. A court-martial is conducted by commissioned officers for soldiers and other members of the armed forces who are under military jurisdiction.

FARRIER: A person who shoes horses.

FLUE: A tube that carries hot gas through a boiler in order to heat the surrounding water in the boiler and generate steam.

GANGPLANK: A wood ramp used to move passengers and freight onto and off a boat.

HOLD: A cargo space beneath the main deck.

HULL: The main body of a ship.

HURRICANE DECK: The deck above the cabin deck. The texas deck and its cabin rest on top of this deck.

JACK STAFF: A pole at the point of the bow that aids the pilot in navigating by providing a reference point that can be aligned with a fixed object on land.

MAIN DECK: The large deck closest to the water.

PACKET: A sail- or steam-powered boat that carried passengers and cargo and ran on a regular schedule between specific cities.

PADDLE WHEEL: A large wheel fitted with flat paddles that propels a steamboat in the water.

PILOTHOUSE: The small, enclosed structure at the top of a steamboat from which the captain or pilot steers the boat and gives orders to the engineers.

RUDDER: A piece of wood or metal that is attached as a blade under the stern of a boat to steer the boat.

SMOKESTACK: A chimney.

STATEROOM: A small room where passengers or officers slept.

STERN: The back of a boat.

SUTLER: A civilian who is authorized to sell goods at a military post.

TEXAS DECK: The deck of a steamboat that contains the officers' quarters.

TILLER: A lever that moves a boat's rudder from side to side.

WESTERN RIVERS: The Mississippi, Ohio, Missouri, and Red Rivers and their tributaries. Together, they form an interconnected waterway system throughout much of the interior of the United States.

WHEELHOUSE: The wooden structure that encloses a steamboat's paddle wheel.

YAWL: A small rowboat kept aboard most steamboats that was used for carrying lines ashore, putting out buoys, or general utility work.

SOURCE NOTES

CHAPTER 1: STEAMBOATS A-COMIN'

p. 1: The name "Mississippi" . . . "a big river": *Ojibwe People's Dictionary,* http://ojibwe.lib .umn.edu.

p. 1: rivers and streams . . . funnel into its channel: "The Mississippi/Atchafalaya River Basin (MARB)," U.S. Environmental Protection Agency website, http://www.epa.gov/ms-htf /mississippiatchafalaya-river-basin-marb.

p. 1: "crookedest river in the world . . . six hundred and seventy-five": Twain, p. 1.

p. 3: "The water was alwaies muddie . . . streame brought downe": Rye, p. 92.

p. 4: "trackless forest . . . by the snake and the alligator": Lanman, p. 113.

pp. 7–8: Yet stumbling blocks . . . boats they needed themselves: Hunter, p. 130.

p. 9: Shreve had ideas for an even better boat . . . than the entire *Enterprise*: Ibid., p. 89.

pp. 9–10: an eyebrow-raising innovation . . . travel the same route: Ibid., pp. 17 and 22.

p. 11: By 1819 . . . western rivers: Ibid., p. 13.

p. 11: That number increased . . . one hundred miles per day: Hall, p. 216, and Hunter, p. 22.

p. 11: By 1848 . . . more than fifteen thousand miles: Kane, *Western River Steamboat,* p. 50.

p. 11: between 1845 and 1855 . . . one hundred steamboats per year: Kane, "Western River Steamboat," p. 58.

p. 11: 2,596 steamboats on western rivers: United States War Department, p. 364.

p. 12: On April 15, President Lincoln issued a proclamation . . . states that had seceded: Abraham Lincoln Papers at the Library of Congress, ser. 1, General Correspondence, 1833–1916, Abraham Lincoln, Monday, April 15, 1861 (Proclamation on State Militia).

CHAPTER 2: OFF TO WAR

p. 13: Eighteen-year-old Michael Dougherty . . . in August 1862: Samuel P. Bates, p. 1306.

p. 15: "for several hours . . . the position of Union forces": Dougherty, p. 73, and "Dougherty, Michael," Congressional Medal of Honor Society website, www.cmohs.org/recipient -detail/379/dougherty-michael.php.

p. 15: Robert Hamilton was born . . . last Confederate state to do so: Frederick H. Dyer, *A Compendium of the War of the Rebellion* (Des Moines, IA: Dyer, 1908), p. 11.

p. 16: "one of the men mounted her . . . without any saddle": Southern Claims Commission Approved Claims, 1871–1880, Robert N. Hamilton file, no. 15627, National Archives and Records Administration, record group 217, https://fold3.com/search/#query=robert+n+hamilton&preview=1&cat=249.

pp. 17–18: Thirteen-year-old Stephen Gaston . . . sent the men to bed at night: Norton, p. 323.

p. 18: "with a brick-red beard": Elliott, p. 84.

pp. 18–19: "delivered to their former masters . . . claimed to own them": *Official Records of the Union and Confederate Armies in the War of the Rebellion*, ser. 2, vol. 8, pp. 175–176.

p. 19: "that every white person . . . discretion of the court": Ibid., p. 800.

p. 19: "Never . . . disclose my identity to friend or foe": J. Walter Elliott in Berry, p. 112.

p. 20: "hearts choicest treasure": Ely, June 16, 1864.

p. 20: "Today I commence . . . may reach her safe": Ibid., June 1, 1864.

p. 21: "Bully for old Abe": Ibid., November 9, 1864.

p. 21: When Ely had free time . . . fine and very tasty: Ibid., June 6, June 12, and July 5, 1864.

p. 21: "No letters yesterday . . . most dear to me": Ibid., August 28, 1864.

p. 21: He welcomed a box . . . worried him greatly: Ibid., October 5, 1864.

p. 21: "very hot, hot, hot!": Ibid., June 26, 1864.

pp. 23–24: "It is hard on our men . . . against us at once": *War of the Rebellion: A Compilation of the Official Records of the Union and Confederate Armies*, ser. 2, vol. 7, p. 607.

p. 24: "We ought not . . . a war of extermination": Ibid., pp. 614–615.

p. 24: At Camp Douglas . . . between 1862 and 1865: Levy, p. 290.

CHAPTER 3: DENS OF DEATH

p. 27: The finished enclosure . . . 779 feet wide: National Park Service website, http://www.nps.gov/ande/learn/historyculture/camp_sumter_history.htm.

p. 27: Camp Sumter Prison . . . ten thousand men: National Park Service, Andersonville National Historic Site website, http://www.nps.gov/ande/learn/index.htm.

p. 28: "for I am tired . . . four or five days": Dougherty, p. 28.

p. 28: "neared the wall . . . nearly all of us forever": Ibid., p. 29.

p. 28: Dougherty and three of his comrades . . . from the cold: Ibid., p. 32.

p. 28: "one of the prisoners . . . caved in on him": Ibid., p. 35.

p. 28: "There is scarcely . . . bare feet": Ibid., p. 33.

pp. 28–29: "The rebels wash . . . filth of all kinds": Ibid., p. 39.

pp. 29–30: "There are millions . . . beside catching gray-backs": Ibid., p. 43 and p. 15.

p. 31: "One Irish potato . . . 25 cents": William McFarland in Berry, p. 248.

p. 31: (Converted into equivalent . . . $3.75): Conversions of monetary values are from Measuring Worth, http://www.measuringworth.com/.

p. 31: "good United States money": William McFarland in Berry, p. 248.

p. 31: During the war . . . end of the war: Hawes, p. 123.

p. 31: "There is a great deal of stealing . . . cause of it all": Dougherty, p. 19.

p. 32: "It has been eight months . . . a mere skeleton": Ibid., p. 41.

p. 32: "by inches . . . a thousand deaths": Ibid., p. 8.

p. 32: News . . . distressed him: Ibid., p. 39.

p. 32: "I will keep up . . . life left in me": Ibid., p. 41.

p. 32: By August . . . capacity: Andersonville Map and Guide, National Park Service, Andersonville National Historic Site website, http://www.nps.gov/ande/planyourvisit/upload/ande_mapandguide-2013.pdf.

p. 32: "hold of a new pencil . . . an inch long": Dougherty, p. 62.

pp. 32–33: "I feel no better . . . when I commenced": Ibid., p. 66.

p. 33: "hungry, dirty, sleepy, and lousy . . . loved ones?": Ely, December 25, 1864.

pp. 33–34: "men die every day . . . a smoke house": Ibid., January 26, 1865.

p. 34: "had a big time washing": Ibid., February 4, 1865.

p. 34: "much depressed . . . weighs heavy": Ibid., February 12, 1865.

p. 34: "some scalawag . . . 4 days rations": Ibid., February 22, 1865.

p. 34: "moving rapidly . . . is my prayer": Ibid., February 28, 1865.

p. 34: "selling chances to leave . . . in [the] first squad": Ibid., March 22, 1865.

p. 35: $80 . . . in twenty-first-century dollars: Conversions of monetary values are from Measuring Worth, http://www.measuringworth.com/.

p. 35: "Peach and cherry trees all in full bloom outside": Ely, March 24, 1865.

p. 35: "How each of us laughed . . . 'Rally Round the Flag, Boys'": J. Walter Elliott in Berry, pp. 113–114.

p. 36: Originally created . . . held three thousand: Hawes, p. 155.

pp. 36–37: One prisoner . . . each man at Cahaba: Ibid., p. 160.

p. 37: men slept on bunks . . . on the ground: Ibid., p. 15.

p. 37: "half a pint . . . all being ground together": "A *Sultana* Survivor," *Elyria (OH) Democrat,*
May 21, 1890, p. 3.

p. 37: "once in ten days . . . [corn]meal": Truman Smith in Berry, p. 323.

pp. 37–39: "We had to do our cooking . . . get out of prison": Ben G. Davis in Berry, p. 103.

p. 39: During March and April . . . occupied the camp: Potter, "The *Sultana* Disaster," p. 11.

p. 40: "All along the road . . . and many little ones": Ely, March 25, 1865.

p. 40: "Oh, this is the brightest day of my life long to be remembered": Ibid., March 31, 1865.

p. 41: "Oh, how I wish I would hear from Julia . . . than anything else": Ibid., April 13, 1865.

p. 41: "Our hearts leaped . . . soon being home]": Arthur A. Jones in Berry, p. 190.

p. 41: "It did my very soul good . . . desire its protection": Stephen Gaston in Berry, p. 149.

p. 41: "Thank God": Ibid., p. 150.

pp. 41–42: "[We] ravenously devoured . . . We feasted on pickles": J. Walter Elliott in Berry,
pp. 114–115.

p. 42: "Lee has caved to Grant, bully, bully, glorious bully": Ely, April 13, 1865.

p. 42: "Bully may we soon see our sweethearts": Ibid., April 14, 1865.

CHAPTER 4: A LARGE AND SPLENDID STEAMER

p. 43: Nearly one-fourth of the steamboats . . . near Cincinnati: Geoffrey J. Giglierano,
Bicentennial Guide to Greater Cincinnati (Cincinnati: Cincinnati Historical Society,
1988), 2:338.

p. 44: Litherbury employees sawed . . . forty-two-foot-wide hull: Descriptions of the *Sultana*
are from "River News," *Cincinnati Daily Commercial,* January 5, 1863, p. 4, and
February 4, 1863, p. 4.

p. 47: To prevent sparks . . . extra-tall smokestacks: Gene Eric Salecker, personal communication to author, August 13, 2015.

p. 48: "large and splendid steamers, designed for the New Orleans trade": *Cincinnati Daily
Commercial,* January 5, 1863, p. 4.

pp. 47–48: "neat, tasty, capacious, and finely furnished": Ibid., February 4, 1863, p. 4.

p. 48: Chandeliers hung . . . in the ladies' cabin: A. C. Brown in Berry, p. 78.

p. 49: "magnificent craft . . . anticipate an agreeable trip": *Cincinnati Daily Commercial,*
February 4, 1863, p. 4.

p. 49: Captain Lodwick considered . . . money well spent: Ibid.

pp. 49–52: lifesaving equipment . . . run ashore: Gene Eric Salecker, personal communication to author, December 17, 2015.

p. 52: By the first week in February 1863 . . . its maiden voyage: Way, p. 436.

p. 52: In May 1863 . . . at Louisville, Kentucky: Rutter, "Bewitching News," p. 12.

p. 53: "wounding 12 or 14 [soldiers], some seriously.": *Official Records of the Union and Confederate Navies in the War of the Rebellion*, p. 4.

p. 53: the *Sultana* . . . traveled to New Orleans: *Times-Picayune* (New Orleans, LA), January 6, 1864, p. 2, and April 15, 1864, p. 4.

p. 53: "The upper works . . . one person was injured": *Cincinnati Enquirer,* August 7, 1863, p. 4.

p. 53: At summer's end . . . to Cairo, Illinois: "News from Southern Illinois," *New York Daily Herald,* August 3, 1863, p. 4.

p. 53: he got married later that year: Charles Theodore Greve, *Centennial History of Cincinnati and Representative Citizens* (Chicago: Biographical Publishing Company, 1904), 2:869–870.

p. 53: Mason . . . two large steamboats: "The *Sultana* Disaster," *Cincinnati Enquirer,* May 2, 1865, p. 4.

p. 54: Mary Rowena Dozier . . . bore his daughter's name: Hyde and Conard, pp. 595–596.

p. 55: "not occupied . . . and infested with rebels": *Official Records of the Union and Confederate Navies,* pp. 335, 336.

p. 56: By the end of April . . . from New Orleans to Cairo: *Joliet (IL) Signal,* April 5, 1864, p. 2.

p. 56: The next month . . . from St. Louis to Little Rock, Arkansas: "Arkansas River News," *Times-Picayune* (New Orleans, LA), May 24, 1864, p. 4.

CHAPTER 5: FREEDOM

p. 57: On April 13, 1865 . . . from St. Louis for New Orleans: *Cincinnati Enquirer,* April 13, 1865, p. 4.

p. 57: "the middle of the inky black night": Twain, p. 107.

p. 59: On the *Sultana*'s last two trips . . . and again at Natchez: Potter, "The *Sultana* Disaster," p. 11.

p. 59: Later that day . . . to half-mast: "Assassination of Lincoln," *National Tribune* (Washington, D.C.), June 7, 1900, p. 7.

p. 61: "Our president . . . true, too true": Ely, April 18, 1865.

p. 61: "Our boys are furious . . . it is a Rebel plot": Dougherty, p. 67.

p. 62: He set a fare . . . adopted by the federal government: Berry, p. 47.

p. 63: "he understood . . . give [Mason] a load": Records of the *Sultana* Disaster, "Proceedings and Report of the Court-Martial of Capt. Frederic Speed," p. 236, http://www.fold3.com/image/249/292470793/.

p. 63: During the third week of April . . . state from which they came: Salecker, p. 35.

p. 63: When the rolls were ready . . . Speed consulted with Colonel Hatch: *War of the Rebellion: A Compilation of the Official Records of the Union and Confederate Armies,* ser. 2, vol. 8, p. 522.

p. 64: Colonel Reuben Hatch . . . military assignments: Potter, *The Sultana Tragedy,* p. 32.

p. 64: In 1862, Hatch had been arrested . . . to gain personal profit: Simon, pp. 325–326.

p. 64: "chartered the steamboat *Keystone* . . . a fee of $1,800": Potter, *The Sultana Tragedy,* p. 35.

p. 64: "frivolous and without the shadow of foundation in fact": Ibid., p. 36.

p. 66: "O[zias] M. Hatch . . . I would like it": Ibid., p. 39.

p. 66: "Hatch was mentally unqualified . . . assistant quartermaster": Ibid., pp. 41–42.

pp. 67–69: After the *Olive Branch* departed . . . could be investigated: Records of the *Sultana* Disaster, "Quartermaster Vessel File," pages 228–232, Washburn Court of Inquiry, testimony of Frederic Speed, https://fold3.com/image/249/292633172/.

p. 68: Map based on map from *Blue & Gray Magazine,* vol. 7, issue 6, p. 10.

p. 69: On April 19 . . . 392 miles away: James, p. 4.

p. 69: Friday morning . . . about three hundred thousand pounds: Potter, "The *Sultana* Disaster," p. 17.

p. 71: Samuel Spikes . . . for a new life upriver: "Terrible Disaster: The Steamer *Sultana* Blown Up — Fourteen Hundred Lives Lost," *Chicago Tribune,* April 28, 1865, p. 1.

p. 71: He wanted the gold stashed . . . all seven were on board: "Appalling Marine Casualty," *Memphis Argus,* April 28, 1865, page number torn off at top.

p. 72: Illinoisan Daniel McLeod . . . at least he still had it: Daniel McLeod in Berry, pp. 254–257.

p. 72: Seth Hardin Jr. . . . December 1864: Seth W. Hardin and Hannah S. Osborne, Cook County, IL, Marriage and Death Indexes, 1833–1889. From *Sam Fink's Chicago Marriage and Death Index*, compiled by Sam Fink, Chicago, IL.

p. 72: That afternoon . . . forty passengers settled in for the ride: Records of the *Sultana* Disaster, "Quartermaster Vessel File," p. 51, Washburn Court of Inquiry, testimony of George Kayton, https://fold3.com/image/249/292632991.

CHAPTER 6: COUNTDOWN TO DISASTER

p. 73: Nathan Wintringer . . . until the boiler was fixed: Records of the *Sultana* Disaster, "Quartermaster Vessel File," p. 48, Washburn Court of Inquiry, testimony of William Rowberry, https://fold3.com/image/249/292632988.

p. 73: "Why did you not have this repaired . . . when the boat left": Records of the *Sultana* Disaster, "Proceedings and Report of the Court-Martial of Capt. Frederic Speed," p. 81, https://fold3.com/image/249/292470520/.

p. 73–74: Taylor favored a large repair . . . he wasn't happy about it: Ibid., p. 84, https://fold3.com/image/249/292470527/.

p. 75: "it would hardly pay . . . number of men": Records of the *Sultana* Disaster, "Quartermaster Vessel Files," p. 139, Dana Court of Inquiry, testimony of Miles Sells, https://fold3.com/image/249/292633079/.

p. 75: "he would give [Mason] . . . bringing in the men [to the wharf]": Records of the *Sultana* Disaster, "Proceedings and Report of the Court-Martial of Capt. Frederic Speed," p. 242, testimony of Miles Sells, https://fold3.com/image/249/292470794.

p. 76: "he could have . . . got ready to go": Records of the *Sultana* Disaster, "Quartermaster Vessel File," p. 230, Washburn Court of Inquiry, testimony of Frederic Speed, https://fold3.com/image/249/292633170/.

p. 77: Between six and seven o'clock . . . prisoners would be forwarded that day: Records of the *Sultana* Disaster, "Proceedings and Report of the Court-Martial of Capt. Frederic Speed," p. 114, https://fold3.com/image/249/292470576/.

p. 77: "the Quartermaster's Department will furnish transportation": Ibid., p. 24, https://fold3.com/image/249/292470425/.

p. 77: With the orders issued . . . Speed was familiar with the process: Ibid., p. 131, https://fold3.com/image/249/292470603/.

p. 78: Meanwhile, Captain William Kerns . . . all the men could go on the *Sultana*: Records of the *Sultana* Disaster, "Quartermaster Vessel File," pp. 195–197, Washburn Court of Inquiry, testimony of William Kerns, https://fold3.com/image/249/292633135/.

p. 79: "placed on board . . . on the Mississippi River": Records of the *Sultana* Disaster, "Proceedings and Report of the Court-Martial of Capt. Frederic Speed," p. 72, https://fold3.com/image/249/292470713.

p. 79: Unbeknownst to Frederic Speed . . . returned from lunch: Salecker, p. 51.

pp. 79–80: Alarmed by the number . . . place some of the men on the *Pauline Carroll*: Records of the *Sultana* Disaster, "Quartermaster Vessel File," p. 196, Washburn Court of Inquiry, testimony of William Kerns, https://fold3.com/image/249/292633136/.

p. 80: "very high over [the] country every where": Ely, April 24, 1865.

p. 80: Water surrounded the barns . . . impossible to see land at all: N. H. Karns, "The Loss of the *Sultana*," *National Tribune* (Washington, D.C.), October 26, 1893, p. 1.

p. 80: "a large but not very fine boat": Ely, April 24, 1865.

p. 80: "stuck together . . . during the war": Arthur A. Jones in Berry, p. 191.

p. 80: they saw Mr. Taylor repairing the boiler: Ibid., p. 190.

p. 81: "a herd of cattle": William Fies in Berry, p. 125.

p. 81: "We marched . . . as thick as bees": Carson Brewer, "A Surviving Soldier Wrote a Description of the *Sultana*'s Sinking," *Knoxville News Sentinel,* May 31, 1981, p. C4.

pp. 82–83: "Would it not be better . . . Let us see about this": Records of the *Sultana* Disaster, "Proceedings and Report of the Court-Martial of Capt. Frederic Speed," p. 104, https://fold3.com/image/249/292470560/.

p. 83: "I have been on board . . . go comfortably": Records of the *Sultana* Disaster, "Quartermaster Vessel File," p. 235, Washburn Court of Inquiry, testimony of Frederic Speed, https://fold3.com/image/249/292633175/.

p. 83: "packed on the boat . . . they all went on board": Ibid., p. 148, testimony of William Butler, https://fold3.com/image/249/292633088/.

p. 84: Kerns, increasingly concerned . . . could do as he chose: Ibid., p. 197, testimony of Frederic Speed, https://fold3.com/image/249/292633137/.

p. 84: Meanwhile, the prisoners finished boarding . . . be careful about fire: Records of the *Sultana* Disaster, "Proceedings and Report of the Court-Martial of Capt. Frederic Speed," p. 40, https://fold3.com/image/1/292470647/, and p. 222, https://fold3.com/image/249/292633162/.

pp. 85–86: Ann and Harvey Annis . . . lieutenant in the Fifty-First U.S. Colored Troops: Jerry O. Potter Collection, Memphis Public Library, box 3, folder 8, and Records of the *Sultana* Disaster, "Quartermaster Vessel File," pp. 152–153, Washburn Court of Inquiry, testimony of Ann Annis, https://fold3.com/image/249/292633092/.

p. 86: "the clerk or mate pointed out . . . only little moving about": Records of the *Sultana* Disaster, "Quartermaster Vessel File," p. 153, testimony of Ann Annis, https://fold3.com/image/249/292633093/.

p. 86: William D. Snow . . . arrive on board until almost 10 p.m.: Ibid., p. 112, testimony of William D. Snow, https://fold3.com/image/249/292633052/.

p. 86: "seventy cabin passengers . . . belonging to the boat" . . . on the *Sultana*: Ibid., p. 113, testimony of William D. Snow, https://fold3.com/image/249/292633053.

p. 86: (Ongoing research indicates . . . 2,400 people on board): Gene Eric Salecker, personal communication to author, August 13, 2015.

p. 87: "bell rang and the wheels began . . . we cheered and shouted": N. H. Karns, "The Loss of the *Sultana*," *National Tribune* (Washington, D.C.), October 26, 1893, p. 2.

p. 87: The journey from Vicksburg to Memphis . . . cooking in shifts: Potter, "The *Sultana* Disaster," p. 17.

p. 88: "housing and meals . . . discharge from the military": LaPointe, p. 339.

p. 88: While in Vicksburg . . . small comforts such as tobacco: Ibid., p. 341.

p. 88: "who pocketed the difference . . . a scoundrelly Quartermaster": "*Sultana* Slaughter," *Indianapolis Daily Journal* 14, no. 263, May 4, 1865, p. 2.

p. 88: "We would punch him . . . in the closet under the stairway": William Lugenbeal in Berry, p. 225.

p. 88: "We were on our way . . . cheered by the thought": Albert W. King in Berry, p. 200.

p. 89: "Mason. . . complained . . . the boilers might explode": Records of the *Sultana* Disaster, "Quartermaster Vessel File," p. 124, Washburn Court of Inquiry, testimony of William S. Friesner, https://fold3.com/image/249/292633064/.

p. 90: Kinser, James Payne . . . barracks, a kitchen, and a dining hall: LaPointe, p. 339.

p. 90: The men were looking for a good meal: "Story of Another Survivor: How James Payne Escaped by Going After a Bite to Eat," *Chicago Daily Tribune*, April 22, 1888, p. 26.

p. 91: "I found a hogshead . . . two pounds of sugar each," Stephen Gaston in Berry, p. 150.

p. 91: Ann Annis slipped a pink nightdress over Isabella's head: *Oshkosh (WI) Daily Northwestern*, March 30, 1888, p. 1.

p. 91: Filled with a good meal . . . not far from where Karns lay: N. H. Karns, "The Loss of the *Sultana*," *National Tribune* (Washington, D.C.), October 26, 1893, p. 2.

p. 92: Walter Elliott . . . a much cooler place to sleep: J. Walter Elliott in Berry, p. 116.

p. 93: "was compelled to crawl around . . . subject of several jokes": William Fies in Berry, p. 126.

p. 93: With the *Sultana*'s paddle wheels churning . . . north to Union army camps: Records of the *Sultana* Disaster, "Quartermaster Vessel File," p. 51, Washburn Court of Inquiry, testimony of George Kayton, https://fold3.com/image/249/292632991.

p. 93: As usual . . . a head of steam rose in the boilers: "The *Sultana*," *Chicago Tribune*, May 5, 1865, p. 2.

p. 93: While the *Sultana* had been refueling . . . two o'clock in the morning: "Story of Another Survivor: How James Payne Escaped by Going After a Bite to Eat," *Chicago Daily Tribune*, April 22, 1888, p. 26.

CHAPTER 7: END OF THE WORLD

p. 94: "Nothing more than common was in progress": "The Awful Disaster to the 'Sultana,'" *California Daily Evening Bulletin*, May 30, 1865, p. 1.

p. 94: Suddenly . . . one of the *Sultana*'s boilers burst: Potter, "The *Sultana* Disaster," p. 8.

p. 95: "was full, a sea of heads for hundreds of yards around": "Statement of Pilot George J. Cayton," *Memphis Argus*, April 28, 1865, page number torn off.

p. 95: During the journey north . . . hauled up water: Gene Eric Salecker, personal communication to author, December 15, 2015.

p. 98: "They were leaping off . . . into the water without sinking": Robert N. Hamilton in Berry, p.165.

p. 99: "When I came to . . . got there to milk her": Jesse Martin in Berry, p. 237.

p. 100: "As I was descending . . . knocked me into the hold" . . . They could use it as a raft: "In a River Wreck," *Oshkosh (WI) Daily Northwestern,* March 30, 1888, p. 1. The narrative of the Annis family's actions during the disaster is based on Ann Annis's interview in the newspaper and on her testimony given to the Washburn Court of Inquiry, https://fold3.com/image/249/292633092/.

pp. 100–102: At the sound of the explosion . . . away from the burning boat and into darkness: J. Walter Elliott in Berry, pp. 117–119, and Daniel McLeod in Berry, pp. 254–256.

p. 103: "Everywhere steam was escaping . . . splinters flying": "The Loss of the *Sultana,*" *National Tribune* (Washington, D.C.), October 26, 1893, p. 2.

p. 103: "on it crashed down . . . on the bow of the boat below": Ibid., p. 2.

p. 104: "crowds from each deck . . . to assist those in the water": Records of the *Sultana* Disaster, "Quartermaster Vessel File," pp. 275–281, Washburn Court of Inquiry, testimony of Jacob Rush, https://fold3.com/image/249/292633215, and Jacob Rush in Hawes, pp. 192–199.

pp. 104–105: "When I got through with my smoke . . . almost walk over their heads": Ben G. Davis in Berry, pp. 103–104.

p. 105: "every loose board . . . and jumped after it": William Lugenbeal in Berry, p. 226.

pp. 105–106: "There isn't any skin left . . . into the flames": William A. McFarland in Berry, pp. 249–250.

p. 106: When chief engineer Nathan Wintringer . . . jumped into the river: Rutter, "Twice Overlooked," p. 11.

p. 106: "raised to a height": Stephen Gaston in Berry, p. 150.

p. 107: "Their cries . . . dark night hideous": Ibid., p. 151.

p. 108: "The glare from the burning boat . . . timber along the banks": Hugh Kinser in Berry, pp. 206–207.

p. 108: "Sometimes I would get . . . back and forth across the river": Joseph H. Mayes in Berry, p. 239.

p. 109: "Coming to a leaning willow . . . I got chilly in that position": Simeon D. Chelf in Berry, pp. 90–91.

p. 109: "I could hear . . . five of us on the log": Ben G. Davis in Berry, p. 104.

p. 110: "All this time . . . be saved?" and "In a few . . . scarcely speak": Albert W. King in Berry, pp. 201–203.

p. 110: "I was chilled to the marrow": N. H. Karns, "The Loss of the *Sultana*" (part 3), *National Tribune* (Washington, D.C.), November 2, 1893, p. 1.

p. 111: "Just a little below us . . . in blisters all over": Ibid.

p. 111: "Imagine my surprise . . . the little one before her": William A. McFarland in Berry, p. 250.

p. 111: "After the dawn of day mosquitoes came on us by the thousands": Simeon D. Chelf in Berry, pp. 89–91.

CHAPTER 8: RESCUE

p. 113: "until the last man was rescued . . . to an immense height": Hugh Kinser in Berry, p. 209.

p. 113: For hours more, the Foglemans searched . . . near-frozen survivors: Descriptions of the Fogleman family's actions are from Frank Fogleman, personal communication to author, July 17, 2015; *Memphis Argus*, April 28, 1865; and Robert Hamilton in Berry, p. 166.

p. 113: The Fogleman family is credited with saving about one hundred lives: "Terrible Disaster: The Steamer *Sultana* Blown Up — Fourteen Hundred Lives Lost," *Chicago Tribune*, April 28, 1865, p. 1.

p. 113–115: "the two men that rescued us . . . no less than thirty lives": "Appalling Marine Casualty," *Memphis Argus*, April 28, 1865, page number torn off.

p. 115: "A steamboat is afire . . . in plain view of my mother and me": "Sunday Is Anniversary of *Sultana* Explosion," *West Memphis Evening Times*, April 25, 1969, p. 10. The description of the Berrys' experience is based on Louis's account in this article.

p. 115: "with both legs broken . . . and was seen no more": *Memphis Daily Bulletin*, April 28, 1865, p. 2.

p. 116: Louis's mother brought a big pot . . . shake the Berrys' house down: Ogilvie E. Hamblin in Berry, p. 163.

p. 116: "he did not care . . . do all in his power to help them": "Going In for Humanity," *Memphis Argus*, April 28, 1865, page number torn off, and author interview with Frank Barton, descendant of Franklin Barton, July 17, 2015.

p. 117: "drew a ring from her finger . . . as a token of reward": Albert W. King in Berry, pp. 203–204.

p. 117: On the Tennessee shore . . . collected, possibly identified, and buried: "The Terrible Steamboat Disaster," *Chicago Tribune*, May 1, 1865, p. 2.

p. 117: Surrounded by dense early-morning fog . . . might never find them: W. H. Michael, "*Sultana* Explosion," *National Tribune* (Washington, D.C.), July 26, 1888, p. 2.

p. 118: "Our yawl made nine trips . . . from four to five persons": Records of the *Sultana* Disaster, "Quartermaster Vessel File," p. 118, Washburn Court of Inquiry, testimony of William B. Alwood, https://www.fold3.com/image/249/292633059.

p. 118: "did not cease his efforts . . . any found needing assistance": W. P. Madden in Berry, p. 233.

p. 118: "We also used our lines in bringing persons to the boat": "The *Sultana* Disaster," *Daily National Intelligencer* (Washington, D.C.), May 5, 1865 (reprinted from *Memphis Daily Bulletin,* April 28, 1865).

p. 119: But Captain Watson realized . . . that more help was needed: Records of the *Sultana* Disaster, "Quartermaster Vessel File," pp. 118–119, Washburn Court of Inquiry, testimony of William B. Alwood, https://fold3.com/image/249/292633058.

p. 119: "clutched the limb . . . upon the surface of the river": W. H. Michael, "*Sultana* Explosion," *National Tribune* (Washington, D.C.), July 26, 1888, p. 2.

p. 120: "I heard the cries . . . calling for help": Thomas C. Love in Berry, p. 222.

p. 120: "I ordered. . . to the middle of the river": James Berry's account is from the *Memphis Argus,* April 28, 1865, page number torn off, and *War of the Rebellion: A Compilation of the Official Records of the Union and Confederate Armies,* ser. 1, vol. 48, pt. 1, pp. 220–223.

p. 120: "The shrieks of the wounded . . . were the only guide we had": *War of the Rebellion: A Compilation of the Official Records of the Union and Confederate Armies,* ser. 1, vol. 48, pt. 1, p. 220.

pp. 121–122: "Before we had taken in half . . . came whistling over our heads": Ibid., p. 221.

p. 122: "All that day . . . saved from a watery grave": Thomas C. Love in Berry, p. 223.

p. 123: By noon on April 27 . . . more were on the way to shore: "Appalling Marine Casualty," *Memphis Argus,* April 28, 1865, page number torn off.

p. 123: Although the sentries . . . the company surgeon attended to them: *War of the Rebellion: A Compilation of the Official Records of the Union and Confederate Armies,* ser. 1, vol. 48, pt. 1, p. 223.

p. 123: As the day wore on . . . were taken to Memphis's wharf: Potter, "The *Sultana* Disaster," p. 24.

CHAPTER 9: A GRIM SEARCH

p. 124: "linen and cotton for bandages": LaPointe, p. 330.

p. 124: "wept like a school boy": N. H. Karns, "The Loss of the *Sultana*" (part 3), *National Tribune* (Washington, D.C.), November 2, 1893, p. 1.

p. 125: "was so horribly scalded . . . skin was left on the whole body": Potter, "The *Sultana* Disaster," p. 24.

p. 126: Burned and exhausted, Ann Annis lay helpless in Overton Hospital: "Appalling Marine Casualty," *Memphis Argus,* April 28, 1865, page number torn off, and "More About the *Sultana* Explosion," *Memphis Argus,* April 29, 1865, page number torn off.

p. 126: She prayed . . . the soldier had seen her family: "In a River Wreck," *Oshkosh (WI) Daily Northwestern,* March 30, 1888, p. 1.

p. 127: "an old pair of pants . . . belonged to an artilleryman": N. H. Karns, "The Loss of the *Sultana*" (part 3), *National Tribune* (Washington, D.C.), November 2, 1893, p. 1.

p. 127: "it was no use . . . cut it off above the old wound": Daniel McLeod in Berry, pp. 256–257.

p. 128: "so as to keep [my] clothes clean": Simeon D. Chelf in Berry, p. 91.

pp. 128–130: There Elliott met George Safford . . . and was reunited with his father: The descriptions of Elliott's search with Safford and of Elliott's revelation of his identity are based on J. Walter Elliott in Berry, pp. 122–123, and Elliott, p. 185.

p. 130: "I am one of the lucky ones . . . great joy": Dougherty, pp. 70–71.

p. 130: found Elethia Spikes's family Bible . . . twelve members of the family: "Terrible Disaster: The Steamer *Sultana* Blown Up — Fourteen Hundred Lives Lost," *Chicago Tribune*, April 28, 1865, p. 1.

pp. 130–131: The day after the explosion . . . transported to Memphis: Salecker, p. 187.

p. 131: A weakened Seth Hardin . . . looked bedraggled: "Two Pictures," *Cincinnati Enquirer*, May 5, 1865, p. 2, and "The *Sultana* Disaster," *Daily National Intelligencer* (Washington, D.C.), May 5, 1865 (reprinted from *Memphis Daily Bulletin*, April 28, 1865, p. 2).

p. 131: "reward notice . . . for the recovery of his wife's body": Potter, *The Sultana Tragedy*, p. 128.

pp. 131–132: "could see tears . . . when he would pick up a body": "Another Search After the *Sultana*," *Memphis Argus*, May 13, 1865, page number torn off.

p. 132: For days and weeks . . . left the bodies where they were: Charles Ackley, *Log of* USS *Tyler*, p. 110, Public Library of Cincinnati and Hamilton County, OH.

p. 132: "The most horrible sight . . . dead bodies from the *Sultana*": Phineas D. Parks, "The *Sultana* Disaster," *National Tribune*, January 3, 1889, p. 6.

pp. 132–133: Identifying the victims . . . otherwise have been identified: "Afternoon Telegraph. From Cairo and Below — Important Military Orders," *Chicago Tribune*, May 11, 1865, p. 2.

p. 133: Major William Fidler . . . could keep the two gold items: "Maj. W. H. Fidler, 6 Kentucky Cavalry," *Memphis Argus*, May 9, 1865, no page number.

p. 133: Rumors also circulated about Cass Mason . . . offered for his body: Salecker, pp. 186–187.

p. 134: "and made a diligent search . . . to discover or hear anything of him.": *Times-Picayune* (New Orleans, LA), May 6, 1865, p. 1.

p. 134: At least one person . . . made plans to go up and investigate: "The *Sultana* Explosion — Some New Developments," *Memphis Argus*, April 30, 1865, p. 3.

p. 134: Burying the dead . . . near the *Sultana*'s charred hull: "Investigation of the *Sultana* Disaster," *Memphis Argus,* May 11, 1865, no page number.

p. 134: Two years later . . . washed away the names: Amanda Rhodes (National Cemetery Memphis), personal communication to author, July 16, 2015.

p. 136: The mayor of Memphis housed survivors . . . also paid their hotel bills: "The *Sultana* Explosion — Some New Developments," *Memphis Argus,* April 30, 1865, p. 3.

p. 136: a total of $1,183.90 (about $17,700 in modern currency): Conversions of monetary values are from Measuring Worth, http://www.measuringworth.com/.

p. 136: DeWitt Spikes was given $200; Daniel McLeod was given $100: "Relief Fund for the Sufferers by the *Sultana* Disaster," *Memphis Argus,* May 27, 1865, no page number.

p. 136: "who was left alone . . . as husband, child, and sister were lost": "The *Sultana* Disaster," *Daily National Intelligencer* (Washington, D.C.), May 5, 1865 (reprinted from *Memphis Daily Bulletin,* April 28, 1865).

p. 137: "The thoughts of getting on another boat . . . on another boat" and "I made my way to . . . reached Cairo the next day": N. H. Karns, "The Loss of the *Sultana*" (part 3), *National Tribune* (Washington, D.C.), November 2, 1893, p. 1.

p. 137: "I dreaded getting on a steamboat . . . explosion was about to take place": William A. McFarland in Berry, pp. 251–252.

p. 137: "a large, fine looking . . . gave one to each of us": N. W. Gregory in Berry, p. 157.

p. 138: (In modern currency, this would be the equivalent of about $15): Conversions of monetary values are from Measuring Worth, http://www.measuringworth.com/.

p. 138: "On arriving at Mattoon . . . the stoutest hearts on that occasion": Robert N. Hamilton in Berry, pp.166–167.

p. 138: "dinner worthy of my grand old native state": J. Walter Elliott in Berry, p. 124.

pp. 138–139: "No more screeching of shells . . . I was safe at home": N. H. Karns, "The Loss of the *Sultana*" (part 3), *National Tribune* (Washington, D.C.), November 2, 1893, p. 1.

p. 139: In a report dated May 19, 1865 . . . the total lost . . . was 1,238: Records of the *Sultana* Disaster, "Quartermaster Vessel File," p.105, William Hoffman to Edwin Stanton, https://fold3.com/image/249/292633045.

p. 139: "Burned [on the Mississippi] and 1,600 persons perished": Way, p. 436.

CHAPTER 10: WHY?

p. 140: In the wake of the horrendous disaster . . . it exploded?: Records of the *Sultana* Disaster, "Quartermaster Vessel File," pp. 130–132, Washburn Court of Inquiry, testimonies of William Postal and John Curtis, https://www.fold3.com/image/249/292633070.

p. 140: "a certain eternally-infamous villain . . . the *Sultana*": "The Explosion of the *Sultana* — A Rebel Plot," *Cleveland Daily Leader,* May 3, 1865, p. 2.

p. 141: "a torpedo . . . must have caused the explosion": *Findlay (OH) Jeffersonian,* May 5, 1865, p. 2.

pp. 141–142: "beyond a doubt . . . was the cause of the explosion": "Investigation of the *Sultana* Disaster," *Memphis Argus,* May 11, 1865, no page number.

p. 142: "notorious Confederate . . . blockade-runner": "Is the Mystery Solved?" *Chicago Tribune,* May 7, 1888, p. 2.

p. 142: "in front of the boilers for . . . the destruction of the boat": "The *Sultana* Explosion," *Atchison (KS) Daily Champion,* May 8, 1888.

p. 142: "The greatest care was exercised . . . some fiendish effort would be made": "Current Bits of Gossip," *Chicago Tribune,* May 13, 1888, p. 26.

p. 143: "considered the boilers safe . . . her being very light": Records of the *Sultana* Disaster, "Quartermaster Vessel File," p. 118, Washburn Court of Inquiry, testimony of Samuel Clemens, https://fold3.com/image/249/292633058.

p. 144: "Not having [Tillinghast's] measure, he had made it all right anyhow": Ibid., p. 138, Dana Commission, testimony of James McGuire, https://www.fold3.com /image/249/292633078.

p. 145: the secretary of war . . . issue a report directly to him: *War of the Rebellion: A Compilation of the Official Records of the Union and Confederate Armies,* ser. 1, vol. 48, pt. 2, p. 247.

p. 146: "have all parties guilty . . . proper punishment may be had": Ibid., p. 45, Edwin Stanton to Cadwallader Washburn, April 30, 1865, https://fold3.com/ image/249/292470460.

p. 147: "The infernal machine . . . for the transportation of the troops": "The *Sultana* Tragedy," *Chicago Tribune,* May 5, 1865, p. 2.

p. 147: "It cannot be pleaded . . . regard to his wealth or position": "The *Sultana* Disaster," *Shreveport (LA) Weekly News,* May 13, 1865, p. 2.

p. 148: The average air pressure . . . 14.7 pounds per square inch: "Basic Climatological Information and Definitions," International Research Institute for Climate and Society website, http://iridl.ldeo.columbia.edu/dochelp/QA/Basic/atmos_press.html.

pp. 148–149: At the *Sultana*'s inspection . . . 145 pounds of pressure per square inch: Records of the *Sultana* Disaster, "Proceedings and Report of the Court-Martial of Capt. Frederic Speed," p. 3, inspector's certificate, https://fold3.com/image/249/292470392.

p. 149: Under that pressure, water boils at 363° F (184° C): Patrick Jennings, Hartford Steam Boiler company blog, "The *Sultana* — Part 2: How Do Boilers Go Boom?," http://blog .hsb.com/2015/04/06/sultana-boiler-explosion/#comments.

p. 149: Nathan Wintringer . . . a pressure of 130 to 135 pounds: Records of the *Sultana* Disaster, "Proceedings and Report of the Court-Martial of Capt. Frederic Speed," p. 286, https://fold3.com/image/249/292470867.

p. 149: According to Wintringer . . . it was fairly large: Ibid., p. 284, https://fold3.com /image/249/292470864.

p. 151: "This report reads . . . and not hurt their feelings": "The *Sultana* Disaster," *Chicago Tribune*, May 24, 1865, p. 2.

p. 152: "neglect of duty . . . good order and military discipline": Records of the *Sultana* Disaster, "Proceedings and Report of the Court-Martial of Capt. Frederic Speed," p. 13, https://fold3.com/image/249/292470409.

p. 154: Lieutenant Tillinghast . . . a jail sentence for forgery: Salecker, p. 198.

CHAPTER 11: A SAD TRUTH

p. 157: "About two or three months . . . killed upon the 'Sultana'": Berry, pp. 55–56.

pp. 158–159: In 1890, Marcellus Reynolds . . . survivors to respond: "A *Sultana* Survivor," *Elyria (OH) Democrat*, May 21, 1890, p. 3.

p. 159: "There is a kindred feeling . . . that shall bind us together": "Dr. Madden Talks," *Xenia (OH) Daily Gazette*, June 18, 1890, p. 1.

p. 159: Private Charles Eldridge . . . at age ninety-six: Gene Eric Salecker, personal communication to author, December 15, 2015.

p. 161: More than 750,000 men had died as a direct result of the war: Hacker, p. 348.

EPILOGUE

p. 163: "leaving Vicksburg high and dry": Wayman, p. 98.

p. 163: In the area where the *Sultana* sank . . . since April 27, 1865: Berryman, Potter, and Oliver, p. 848.

p. 163: "most distinguished gallantry . . . October 12, 1863": Dougherty, p. 73.

p. 164: "better able to appreciate the many blessings you now enjoy": Ibid., p. 71.

p. 165: Residents of Mound City . . . poking up through the soil: Frank Barton, personal communication to author, July 17, 2015.

AUTHOR'S NOTE

p. 168: Two-fifths of all soldiers . . . at the time they enlisted: Hacker, 330.

BIBLIOGRAPHY

Bates, Alan L. *The Western Rivers Steamboat Cyclopoedium*. Leonia, NJ: Hustle Press, 1968.

Bates, Samuel P. *History of Pennsylvania Volunteers, 1861–5,* Vol. 5. Harrisburg, PA: B. Singerly, 1870. https://archive.org/details/histpennavol05baterich.

Berry, Chester D., ed. *Loss of the Sultana and Reminiscences of Survivors.* 1892. Reprint, Knoxville: University of Tennessee Press, 2005.

Berryman, Hugh, Jerry O. Potter, and Samuel Oliver. "The Ill-fated Passenger Steamer *Sultana." Journal of Forensic Sciences 33*, no. 3 (May 1988): 848.

Bragg, Marion. *Historic Names and Places on the Lower Mississippi River*. Vicksburg: Mississippi River Commission, 1977. http://www.mvd.usace.army.mil/Portals/52 /docs/MRC/MRnames(Intro-end_final2).pdf.

Bryant, William O. *Cahaba Prison and the Sultana Disaster*. Tuscaloosa: University of Alabama Press, 1990.

Carter, Hodding. *The Rivers of America: Lower Mississippi*. New York: Farrar & Rinehart, 1942.

Dougherty, Michael. *Prison Diary of Michael Dougherty, Late Co. B, 13th Pa., Cavalry.* Bristol, PA: Chas. A. Dougherty, 1908. http://publicdomainreview.org/collections/ prison-diary-of-michael-dougherty-1908/.

Drago, Harry Sinclair. *The Steamboaters: From the Early Side-Wheelers to Big Packets.* New York: Bramhall House, 1967.

Elliott, James W. *Transport to Disaster*. New York: Holt, Rinehart and Winston, 1962.

Ely, John Clark. Diary of John C. Ely, 115th Ohio Volunteer Infantry, June 1, 1864–April 26, 1865. Unpublished diary, courtesy of Jerry O. Potter.

Fremling, Calvin R. *Immortal River: The Upper Mississippi in Ancient and Modern Times.* Madison: University of Wisconsin Press, 2005.

Gandy, John W., and Thomas H. Gandy. *The Mississippi Steamboat Era in Historic Photographs: Natchez to New Orleans 1870–1920.* New York: Dover, 1987.

Gould, E. W. *Fifty Years on the Mississippi; or, Gould's History of River Navigation.* 1889. Reprint, Columbus, OH: Long's College Book Company, 1951.

Gourley, Catherine. *The Horrors of Andersonville: Life and Death Inside a Civil War Prison.* Minneapolis: Twenty-First Century Books, 2010.

Hacker, J. David. "A Census-Based Count of the Civil War Dead." *Civil War History* 57, no. 4 (December 2011): 307–348.

Hall, James. *The West: Its Commerce and Navigation.* Cincinnati: H. W. Derby, 1848. https://archive.org/stream/westitscommerce00hallgoog#page/n8/mode/2up.

Hawes, Jesse. *Cahaba: A Story of Captive Boys in Blue.* New York: Burr, 1888.

House of Congress Records for Frances L. Ackley. United States House of Representatives, 57th Congress, 1st Session. Report Number 1160, March 22, 1902, and Report Number 1052, April 10, 1902.

Hunter, Louis C. *Steamboats on the Western Rivers: An Economic and Technological History.* Cambridge, MA: Harvard University Press, 1949.

Hyde, William, and Howard L. Conard, eds. *Encyclopedia of the History of St. Louis.* Vol. 1. St. Louis: Southern History Company, 1899.

James, U. P., 1811–1889. *James' River Guide.* Cincinnati: U. P. James, 1866.

Kane, Adam I. *The Western River Steamboat.* College Station: Texas A&M University Press, 2004.

———. "The Western River Steamboat: Structure and Machinery, 1811 to 1860" (master's thesis, Texas A&M University, May 2001), p. 58. http://nautarch.tamu.edu/pdf-files /Kane-MA2001.pdf.

Lanman, James H. "American Steam Navigation." *Hunt's Merchants' Magazine and Commercial Review* 4 (1841): 105–129. http://catalog.hathitrust.org/Record /000057181.

LaPointe, Patricia M. "Military Hospitals in Memphis, 1861–1865." *Tennessee Historical Quarterly* 42, no. 4 (winter 1983): 325–342.

Latrobe, John H. B. *The First Steamboat Voyage on the Western Waters.* Baltimore: Maryland Historical Society, 1871. http://catalog.hathitrust.org/Record/011262596.

Levy, George. *To Die in Chicago: Confederate Prisoners at Camp Douglas 1862–1865.* Evanston, IL: Evanston Publishing, 1994.

Morrison, John H. *History of American Steam Navigation.* New York: W. F. Sametz, 1903. http://catalog.hathitrust.org/Record/001624262.

Norton, Oliver Willcox. *Army Letters, 1861–1865.* Chicago: O. L. Deming, 1903.

Official Records of the Union and Confederate Navies in the War of the Rebellion. Washington, D.C.: U.S. Government Printing Office, 1908. Reprint, North Carolina: Historical Times, Inc., 1987.

Petersen, William J. "Captains and Cargoes of Early Upper Mississippi Steamboats." *The Wisconsin Magazine of History* 13, no. 3 (March 1930): 224–240.

Potter, Jerry. "The *Sultana* Disaster: Conspiracy of Greed." *Blue & Gray Magazine* 7, issue 6 (1990): 8–24, 54–59.

———. *The Sultana Tragedy: America's Greatest Maritime Disaster*. Gretna, LA: Pelican, 1992.

Records of the *Sultana* Disaster, April 27, 1865. National Archives and Records Administration Catalog Title: *Records of the Sultana Disaster Compiled 1865–1865*. Publication no. M1878, https://fold3.com. Includes the reports of the Washburn, Dana, and Hoffman Commissions, "Quartermaster Vessel File Relating to the *Sultana*," and "Proceedings and Report of the Court-Martial of Capt. Frederic Speed, Court-Martial Case MM3967."

Rutter, J. W. "Bewitching News." *S&D Reflector* 2, no. 3 (September 1965): 12.

———. "Twice Overlooked." *S&D Reflector* 2, no. 2 (June 1965): 10–12.

Rye, William B., ed. The Discovery and Conquest of Terra Florida, by Don Ferdinando de Soto: And Six Hundred Spaniards His Followers, Written by a Gentleman of Elvas, Employed in All the Action, and Translated out of Portuguese, by Richard Hakluyt. 1851 (reprint of 1611 edition). Reprint, Cambridge: Cambridge Library Collection, 2010. http://catalog.hathitrust.org/Record/001166290.

Salecker, Gene Eric. *Disaster on the Mississippi: The Sultana Explosion, April 27, 1865*. Annapolis, MD: Naval Institute Press, 1996.

Simon, John Y., ed. *The Papers of Ulysses S. Grant*. Vols. 3 and 4. Carbondale: Southern Illinois University Press, 1972.

Sneden, Robert Knox. *Eye of the Storm*. Edited by Charles F. Bryan Jr. and Nelson D. Lankford. New York: Free Press, 2000.

Thatcher, Joseph M., and Thomas H. Thatcher. *Confederate Coal Torpedo: Thomas Courtenay's Infernal Sabotage Weapon*. Fredericksburg, VA: Keith Kenerly, 2011.

Twain, Mark. *Life on the Mississippi*. 1883. Reprint, New York: Harper & Brothers, 1903.

United States War Department. Message from the President of the United States to the Two Houses of Congress, 34th Congress, 1st Session, Part 2. Washington, D.C.: Beverly Tucker, 1855.

Wallace, Joseph. *Past and Present of the City of Springfield and Sangamon County Illinois*. Vol. 2. Chicago: S. J. Clarke, 1904.

War of the Rebellion: A Compilation of the Official Records of the Union and Confederate Armies. Washington, D.C.: Government Printing Office, 1880–1891. Ser. 1, vol. 48, pts. 1 and 2; Ser. 2, vol. 8; Ser. 3, vol. 5. Reprint, Harrisburg, PA: National Historical Society, 1971.

Way, Frederick Jr. *Way's Packet Directory 1848–1983*. Athens: Ohio University/Sons and Daughters of Pioneer Rivermen, 1983.

Wayman, Norbury L. *Life on the River: A Pictorial History of the Mississippi, the Missouri, and the Western River System*. New York: Crown, 1971.

FOR FURTHER EXPLORATION

The website of the Association of *Sultana* Descendants and Friends has lots of information about the disaster and interesting links to other sources. http://sultanaremembered.com/.

Steamboats.org has a wealth of information about steamboats and a variety of steam whistles for interested listeners at http://www.steamboats.org/whistle-calliope.html.

To hear some of the many bugle calls that Stephen Gaston had to learn when he served in the Ninth Indiana, visit http://www.secondcavalry.org/bugle_calls.htm.

Blog entries about the *Sultana* explosion written by engineer Patrick Jennings, from the Hartford Steam Boiler Inspection and Insurance Company, include a great video showing how the release of pressure affects a container. http://blog.hsb.com/2015/04/06/sultana-boiler-explosion/.

Patrick Jennings gave a lecture commemorating the 150th anniversary of the explosion. It can be found on YouTube at https://www.youtube.com/watch?v=kEEvcNeizwA. Accessed online October 27, 2015.

IMAGE CREDITS

pp. 3, 5, 17, 22, 27, 29, 30, 33, 41, 61, 65, 74, 75, 120, and 121: Courtesy of the Library of Congress • p. 6: Cincinnati Museum Center (SC#125-010) • p. 8: Courtesy of the Geography and Map Division, Library of Congress • pp. 10, 49, 55, and 71: Courtesy of Special Collections, Murphy Library, University of Wisconsin–La Crosse • p.14: Courtesy of the Michael Dougherty Division #1, Bristol, PA 19007 • p. 15: Courtesy of Kenneth R. Hamilton • p. 19: From Chester D. Berry, ed., *Loss of the Sultana and Reminiscences of Survivors.* 1892. Reprint, Knoxville: University of Tennessee Press, 2005. • p. 20: Courtesy of Maureen Koehl and the Lewisboro Library (New York) • p. 36: From Jesse Hawes, *Cahaba: A Story of Captive Boys in Blue* (New York: Burr, 1888). • p. 38: Courtesy of the National Archives Record Group 107: Records of the Office of the Secretary of War, 1791–1948. War Department, Office of the Secretary, Office of the Military Telegraph. • pp. 40, 62, and 152: From the photo collection of the Old Court House Museum, Vicksburg, MS • p. 42: Courtesy of the National Archives, War Record Group 94: Records of the Adjutant General's Office, 1762–1984. ARC Identifier: 300387. • p. 44: Cincinnati Museum Center (SC#110-185) • p. 45: From the collection of the Public Library of Cincinnati and Hamilton County • p. 47: Diagrams created by Karen Minot based on original diagrams courtesy of Gene Eric Salecker • pp. 48 and 57: From the collections of the St. Louis Mercantile Library at the University of Missouri–St. Louis • p. 50: Courtesy of the National Park Service • p. 52: Courtesy of the Cincinnati History Library and Archives • pp. 54, 90, 92, and 96–97: Courtesy of *Harper's Weekly* • p. 58: Courtesy of the National Archives Record Group 41: Bureau of Marine Inspection and Navigation, Custom House Documents for the port of St. Louis • p. 60: Courtesy of the Alfred Whital Stern Collection, Library of Congress • p. 70: Courtesy of the National Archives Record Group 153: Office of the Judge Advocate General (Army), entry 15 Court Martial Case Files case MM3967, Case of Captain Frederic Speed, box 1494, folder 1. • p. 85: Courtesy of Thomas Mathews, Helen Chandler, the Annis Family Association, and the Memphis and Shelby County Room, Memphis Public Library & Information Center • p. 89: Courtesy of Special Collections, Murphy Library, University of Wisconsin–La Crosse, Historic Steamboat Photographs • p. 122: Courtesy of Missouri History Museum, St. Louis • p. 125: Courtesy of the Memphis and Shelby County Room, Memphis Public Library & Information Center • p. 129: Courtesy of the Cincinnati History Library and Archives • pp. 135 and 160: Courtesy of Sally M. Walker • p. 141: Courtesy of the Courtenay papers, the Thatcher Collection, The American Civil War Museum, Richmond, VA • p. 153: Courtesy of the United States Army Military History Institute, MOLLUS-Mass Volume 97, The U.S. Army Heritage and Education Center, Carlisle, PA

INDEX

Page numbers in italics indicate images or captions.